COLLEGE KNOWLEDGE

Entries into Academic Culture

PAM DUSENBERRY

DUTCH HENRY

T. SEAN RODY

Shoreline Community College
Seattle, Washington

KENDALL/HUNT PUBLISHING COMPANY

4050 Westmark Drive   Dubuque, Iowa 52002

TABLE OF CONTENTS

COLLEGE CULTURE

COLLEGE SUBJECTS

INTRODUCTION

The transition to college from homemaking, work, or high school is a tremendously difficult one. This difficulty is not primarily due, however, to an inability to think critically, take good notes, or develop appropriate study habits. Those, and many other skills, are factors, but not the most critical ones. The most important factor in successfully transitioning into college is the ability to negotiate the culture shock students experience when they enter the academic world. College is a unique culture and community unto itself. It has its own values, beliefs, and behaviors; it has its own ways of thinking, questioning, and communicating. These values can conflict with the values that students hold as they enter the college community. This book seeks to help students understand, appreciate, and participate in college culture.

Students need to be integrated into college culture in order to succeed. This acculturation means learning about the values, behaviors, and sanctions of the academy as well as developing a sense of belonging. Students are in many cases unaware of academic values such as intellectual integrity, hard work, tolerating confusion, respect for evidence, individual initiative, and so on. For example, students perceive the freedom of college to mean they don't have to attend class, they need not arrive on time, and don't need to explain where they have been in either circumstance. While college does bring with it more freedom than high school or the working world, academics do value consistent attendance, timeliness, and a commitment to the work of faculty and other students. As members of the academic community, faculty and staff often perceive students as rejecting those values, when often the reality is the students are unaware of their importance, or ignorant of them altogether. Students need to be introduced to these values in an analytical and critical environment so they can evaluate their benefits and freely choose to participate in the culture of college. In addition, students need to learn how to cope with the dissonance that occurs when the values and behavioral norms of college are different from their home communities and cultures.

Many students also lack an understanding of the academic organization of knowledge and the basic concepts of the disciplines. Academic disciplines see the world in especially unique and structured ways. Disciplines are bound up in rules, codes, discourses, and dynamics that are hidden from the students and largely invisible to the academics who inhabit the college community. What counts as evidence in a chemistry paper, for example, is much different than what counts as evidence in a literary analysis. While students may have a sense that the chemistry paper should be different than the literature paper, the specifics of those differences and the consequences of making a mistake in that distinction is unclear. Students need to be introduced, then, to the differences between the disciplines through an examination of the thinking, questioning, and communicating that occurs.

PART ONE: COLLEGE CULTURE

Part One begins with a poem that illustrates some of the cultures, norms, and values of college. Students have intimate day-to-day knowledge and experience with culture, but rarely examine it in the way this book expects. From that foundation, the readings then introduce students to the many experiences of the members of the campus community. Issues such as grades, attendance, poor instruction, and disruptive classroom behavior are raised in H. Bruce Miller, Tom Wayman, and Peter Sacks. Those combine with discussions of the thinking expected in college, the difficulties in relating home and school, class divisions on campus, and the relationship between contemporary culture and college culture in Christian Zawodniak, bell hooks, and Sacks. Overall, Part One is intended to introduce students to the culture of the college community and invite them to analyze, evaluate, and utilize those cultural elements to better understand and take control of their place within it.

PART TWO: COLLEGE SUBJECTS

Part Two introduces readers to the academic subjects or disciplines and to the larger general education areas such as the physical and natural sciences, the arts and humanities, mathematics, and the social sciences. All academic study occurs within specific subjects or disciplines and structures of thinking; subjects are divided into groups such as the social sciences that share some characteristics. Disciplines ask different questions, investigate different parts of an issue, and emphasize different elements. As Kathleen T. McWhorter so effectively shows in the following example of the dog, each discipline takes a specialized approach to studying the world:

- ◆ An artist might consider the dog as an object of beauty and record its fluid, flexible muscular structure and meaningful facial expressions on canvas.
- ◆ A psychologist might study what human needs are fulfilled by owning a dog.
- ◆ The historian might research the historical importance of dogs...
- ◆ A mathematician might treat the dog as a three-dimensional object comprising planes and angles.
- ◆ A biologist would categorize the dog as *Canis familiaris*. (145)

Students need to be introduced, then, to the point of view, purpose, assumptions, and key concepts of discipline areas.

Another important aspect of college culture is the way that the subjects are organized. When students learn why subjects are organized into larger general education divisions, they gain a deeper understanding of what they are supposed to get out of their undergraduate education. By understanding the nature of scientific investigation or of human expression, students can begin to make connections among the subjects they study and to make better choices about what classes to take and what careers to pursue. The readings in Part Two help students to make better sense of their education.

We have not chosen textbook chapters to introduce students to the academic subjects and their larger groupings. Instead, the readings in this section provide discussions of the key issues within a discipline and provide specific examples of thinking within disciplines. For example, Stephen Jay Gould introduces key concepts within natural science and Deborah Tannen provides insight into social science through a discussion of gendered communication patterns in American culture. Through readings such as these students are introduced to the disciplines and given insight into the specific, focused approaches of each academic area.

A NOTE ON READING INSTRUCTION

Traditionally, reading instruction for college students, especially students who are underprepared for college, has had students learn discrete reading skills such as identifying main ideas and details, defining vocabulary, and so on, in short selections or exercises that are often not clearly related to one other. In this book, the philosophy behind what and how students read is different.

First, the readings here are challenging. They are written for a highly educated audience. We provide readings at this level because students need to develop and practice reading at a level of difficulty similar to what they will encounter in their college classes. Second, the content is carefully chosen to help students understand college culture and the academic subjects. The readings are thus related in meaning and build on each other and help students develop a deeper understanding of ideas and their relationships that serve their current and lifelong learning.

Is it a bad idea to assign very difficult readings to students who might have a hard time understanding them? No, we believe. Students have a difficult time comprehending reading for two general reasons: they don't have sufficient background knowledge, including vocabulary and context, and they don't have adequate or appropriate strategies to attack the reading. If students learn a functional reading process including strategies for solving reading problems, and they are given adequate background knowledge, then they can understand even very difficult material. Another tangible result of choosing challenging material for this type of course is the resulting pride students feel in their intellectual accomplishment.

Rather than providing a great deal of reading apparatus in and around each selected reading in the book, we recommend a consistent reading process we call a "Reading Log." The Reading Log requires readers to pre-read, read, and post-read. Those steps may include the following:

Pre-read

- ◆ Preview—look at the entire reading, looking at headings, chapters, etc.
- ◆ Write down what you anticipate will be in the reading
- ◆ Write questions you have about the subject
- ◆ Write what you already know about the subject

Read

Annotate or write down the following:

- ◆ Questions asked by the author
- ◆ Answers to questions asked by the author
- ◆ Important ideas
- ◆ Main ideas of paragraphs
- ◆ Thesis of the reading
- ◆ Confusing, interesting, troubling, funny, or otherwise noteworthy ideas
- ◆ Words you don't know

Post-read

- ◆ Write down definition of words you didn't know
- ◆ Write a summary paragraph or outline of the reading
- ◆ Write a response to the issues and ideas discussed in the reading

Rather than predetermining the discussion questions for readers, we encourage instructors to allow the students to use their Reading Logs to identify and develop issues, questions, confusions, and problems for discussion. Once they become familiar with the reading process and are given adequate support, they can read better, understand more completely, analyze with depth and detail, and discuss with insight.

SAMPLE ASSIGNMENTS

ASSIGNMENT #1

Understanding the Distribution Areas and the Academic Subjects

The goals of this unit are for you to understand more deeply the distribution areas (DAs) and the subjects in them. In the course of this unit, I hope you will find answers to these questions:

- What makes a particular subject fit within a distribution area?
- What are the fundamental truths or values of the DAs and the subjects?
- What are the major problems or questions addressed in this subject?
- What do people in the field consider to be valid evidence?
- What do people who work in the field actually DO? What abilities are particularly important?
- What kinds of reading does one do in each area?
- What is considered good writing in each area?
- How is knowledge or ability in each subject useful in work? citizenship? friendship? family?

You will be working in groups based on the distribution areas. As a group, you will be responsible for formally presenting your findings to the class at the end of the four-week unit. Between now and then, you will have class time to plan and practice your presentation. In addition, you will write an essay on your subject; this will be an extended definition essay.

In order for you to learn about the DAs and the subject you choose within it, you will do the following:

1. Read a chapter on studying in the various disciplines.
2. Conduct an interview with a faculty member in the field of your choosing.
3. Observe a class in your chosen subject.
4. Survey a textbook used in the class you observe or another class
   in the subject.
5. Research, read, summarize and respond to two longer articles that explore one or two major questions in your subject.
6. Make copies of your log entries on these activities to share with your DA group.
7. Present your findings, with your entire group, to the class.
8. Write an essay based on your learning on your subject.

ASSIGNMENT #2

College Culture and Thought
Distribution Areas and You

OUTCOMES

◆ To develop and use a writing process that includes prewriting, drafting, revising, and editing.
◆ To write an analytical essay that connects your research from your Group Project with your own interests, values, and learning.

Assignment

Write an essay that summarizes and integrates your research on a Distribution Area and subject area with your own interests, values and learning.

- The essay should include references to all three major parts of your research: the class visit, the instructor interview, and the discourse analysis.
- Consider how your subject is related to your DA, the purpose of the subject, why it is studied, why it is important, the major questions asked in the subject, the methods of investigation used, the kinds of evidence used.
- The essay should include references to what you have personally learned through this process.

Pam Dusenberry

Dutch Henry

T. Sean Rody

Shoreline Community College

COLLEGE CULTURE

TOM WAYMAN

DID I MISS ANYTHING?

QUESTION FREQUENTLY ASKED BY
STUDENTS AFTER MISSING A CLASS

Nothing. When we realized you weren't here we sat
with our hands folded on our desks in silence, for the
full two hours

> Everything. I gave an exam worth 40 per cent
> of the grade for this term and assigned some
> reading due today on which I'm about to hand
> out a quiz worth 50 per cent.

Nothing. None of the content of this course has value
or meaning

Take as many days off as you like: any activities we
undertake as a class I assure you will not matter either
to you or me and are without purpose

> Everything. A few minutes after we began last
> time a shaft of light descended and an angel or
> other heavenly being appeared and revealed to
> us what each woman or man must do to attain

divine wisdom in this life and the hereafter

This is the last time the class will meet before we disperse to bring this good news to all people on earth

Nothing. When you are not present how could something significant occur?

Everything. Contained in this classroom is a microcosm of human existence assembled for you to query and examine and ponder

This is not the only place such an opportunity has been gathered

but it was one place

and you weren't here

CHRISTIAN ZAWODNIAK

"I'LL HAVE TO HELP SOME OF YOU MORE THAN I WANT TO":
Teacher Power, Student Pedagogy

Teachers always have power in a class. They hold the grades, and, usually students perceive them as holding the knowledge too. The way teachers use this power is perhaps the defining characteristic of their pedagogy. Some teachers may work with students to create the class environment; others may force a class environment upon students. Regardless of their approach or intent, teachers have the power even before they step into the class. Their syllabus is already made, though not necessarily fixed; students already have perceptions of or attitudes toward the role of the teacher, the course, the school, or maybe even the specific teacher; we students have already been educated throughout our lives on how to treat teachers and how they will treat us. None of this may be explicitly meant by a teacher; perhaps it may not even be implicitly considered but the power is there. This power is no easy burden for teachers: those who ignore lines of power within the class often reinforce them; those who meet power issues by being too controlling often narrow the space for student creativity. A careful balance is hard to achieve, and no one knows how the power issues will play out until class starts.

I write this essay to offer a student perspective on the issues of power in the classroom. And although it is only one perspective, I've done a lot of thinking about teaching styles, about writing, and about conducting classes in my first year of college.

It is the first day of class in my first quarter of freshman English.[1] Jeff, my teacher, has already passed out the syllabus. Some words are spoken, but I don't remember them. Then, from my teacher I hear, "I'll have to help some of you more than I want to." And recall thinking, "This is radical—*not* what I expected." I don't quite understand what Jeff's comment means. It seems rebellious, yet official. Jeff was admitting that teachers, like everyone, get tired. Teachers aren't machines that never run out of energy, but sometimes they have to help students even more than they want to, even when they have been working with students all day. Jeff's directness gave him validity as a person (like us), not a teacher who could do everything. Jeff won't just fit into a teacher "mold," he won't pretend that teachers can just go through a routine; rather he seems like a teacher who will shake things up, breaking that mold.

The course description, directly from the syllabus:

> Since writing is an activity rather than a subject area in itself, you will be learning by doing and becoming more self-aware about what you are now doing and what some of your other options might be. For this reason, much of our time in class will be spent in activities, not in lectures; therefore, it is more than usually important that you come to class faithfully and that you keep up with your assignments.

The syllabus was one of my first impressions of the course. Reading it now, I would say that student awareness of "options" (a word that still means little to me in the syllabus) is the course goal. But Jeff's description seemed

---

1. The purpose of the class was for students to write—we had no literature text, only instruction books, *The Concise Guide to Writing, A Writer's Reference,* and *Re:Visions,* a collection of the best freshman essays from the year before.

so vague to me that I couldn't grasp what the course plan or his vision was. The syllabus didn't tell me what Jeff wanted, but that only intensified Jeff's mystery. He was like a puzzle with dazzling pieces, but not a whole picture could be made out of them. Syllabi are not as revealing as a teacher's day-to-day instruction, so I don't expect too much from a syllabus. However, Jeff didn't expand much on his course description. The most he did was tell us his office hours and office phone number. But the syllabus does show the ideology at work in this case: that students should be left to work by themselves. When teachers leave us students alone, we have the best chances for freedom to find our own voices, and, perhaps, creativity. Our independence allows us to make the class: this was Jeff's silent motto. And it fit perfectly with what he had said on the first day: "I'll have to help some of you more than I want to." Most English teachers often have similar goals—to teach students how to read a text critically or how to write well—but the means and methods of achieving those goals are what count in the classroom, in practice. In my freshman composition class, I experienced the complications of participating in what Jeff considered a "student pedagogy." I am still gaining an understanding of what happened in the class. In this paper, I will show snapshots of the class structure and day-to-day activities. Most of all, I will reflect on what continues to puzzle me most: my affection for the teacher and my shifting views of his attempts at a student-centered pedagogy.

I will start with my first impressions of Jeff and give some of my thoughts of those impressions. Early in the process of writing the paper, I wrote in my journal:

> I think what turned me on to Jeff was what he said in the first week
> of class, and that I wrote at the top of the syllabus: "The five-para-
> graph essay is not only old and silly; it's a rule for a rule's sake."
> Who couldn't love that? It says "break the rules" and it went against
> most of what I had been taught in high school. . . . I also liked Jeff
> 'cause he wore sneakers and jeans and was an inconsistent shaver. I
> guess I saw him as not being a snobby academic—he seemed to fit
> in with us.
>
> —13 February 95

I liked Jeff from the start because of his style. Dressing casually and sitting on a table cast him in the role of "outsider." Of course, his views about the five-paragraph essay, which I knew well from high school, showed that he liked writing for writing's sake, not to fit a formula. Jeff didn't follow the rules; he questioned them. His style seemed to refute the formal power teachers usually show by dressing up or by standing behind a podium giving a lecture.

I also liked things about Jeff's teaching and what he taught. His "scientific method" made sense. When I say scientific method, I do not refer to the formal scientific method used by scientists. I mean that Jeff seemed to think we could and should have what he referred to as a "scientific approach" to writing. When he talked about forms of arguments, he said that there are three basic appeals that arguments can make: to emotions, reason, character. Appeals to emotions, he said, were things like TV commercials. I thought of those fabric softener commercials where the world, and individuals' lives, are bright and sunny, all because of Downy. Jeff plainly stated that appeals to reason were the best kinds of arguments. Arguments about character were what politicians did, but that was my thought, not Jeff's. I didn't use this "thesis triangle," as it was called, in my own writing, but it does show Jeff's scientific pedagogical bent.

Jeff's pedagogy, as I experienced it, was to interfere as little as possible with class activities, leaving the students to run the class. He gave prompts, but once conversation started, he didn't speak. Rather, he would sit there, looking at us or into space, and we would talk and then look at him, looking for some kind of guidance. There was a lot of silence. I didn't think it was good silence usually, but the silence of our uncertainty, intimidation, and confusion. I felt intimidated because we were risking our ideas when we spoke, and the best response we could get from the teacher would be an evaluation—a judgment of our ideas. It wasn't what Jeff did that bothered me—all teachers give prompts and want student participation; it was how he did it that was bad.

Perhaps he thought that in that room, we—students and teacher—could be equals and have an ideal class. However, to achieve the ideal class I think Jeff wanted, students would have needed to leave our experiences with teaching and with the power teachers hold at the door. He wanted students to be observers of the world from his isolated classroom, once saying that to understand a system you have to get outside of it.

But this pedagogy didn't work for the class theme, which was *personal* essays. Students wrote various types of essays: personal experience, profile, problem-solution, concept explanation, but all were to come from our own experiences. In writing personal essays, we go into the world, as observers *and* participants. In my concept paper, for example, I talked about something I knew about. For my profile, I talked about a lady who worked at the cafeteria, because I already had experience with her and impressions of her. I couldn't understand the nuances of preparing for the morning cafeteria rush or of running meal cards through the machine, if I had not known something of her firsthand. For my personal experience paper, I revisited a move from New Jersey to Ohio in third grade. By getting inside that experience, not remaining outside it, I could give rich details. Good writing takes us into a place, and we can't create it by trying to remain outside.

Jeff's method seemed to be based on the assumption that we can't comment on what we do not know and we don't know what we cannot prove. This often meant that he didn't speak much in class, because when we speak we usually make some sort of claim or assertion. He once told us about a student who asserted that the Bible's story of creation was correct, and Jeff said he couldn't prove the student wrong. I took Jeff to mean that we cannot comment on that which we do not know, we can only move to higher levels of probability. Jeff's silence in class discussions, therefore, isn't too surprising. Perhaps he saw silence as an occasion to investigate—and he didn't want to do the investigating for us. He didn't want to do our thinking for us. This approach to teaching resulted in a "laissez-faire" pedagogy. Jeff's job was made easier because he could just watch us work, but it was difficult for me and many of my classmates to understand what he wanted.

As the quarter progressed, I viewed Jeff with admiration, soon joined with intimidation. I began to question his motive for saying he'd probably have to help some of us more than he wanted to. Shouldn't he help us to be as good as we could be? Perhaps, I thought, all teachers have to help some students more than they want to, and of course all teachers get tired. I began to realize how much Jeff's statement reflected both dispassion and fatigue. He didn't give enough constructive guidance. I often felt alone and mean-spirited in the class. In fact, I think I felt alone *because* of the meanspiritedness, which I felt because we students were always subject to Jeff's judgement.

Too often Jeff seemed to present "knowledge" or ask questions of us, and then to assume the role as judge of our ideas. Critical pedagogy teaches that teachers are not the sole possessors of knowledge, and Jeff's pedagogy gave us ourselves to start on. Yet, he did not welcome self-reflection; indeed it usually met with judgement from him. We could speak our minds, but he was still the guard of knowledge, evaluating our responses, rather than encouraging further dialogue.

By presenting and analyzing one particular day in Jeff's class, I can illustrate the intimidating effect of his judgement. On that day Jeff started class by saying something like "How are your papers going?" It wasn't a threatening question, but he spoke in a dispassionate and distant tone. His delivery enacted what he had said on the first day of class: "I'll probably have to help some of you more than I want to."

For a moment, no one spoke. Then I complained that I was having trouble with my concept paper. Specifically, I was having trouble showing my thesis, that football was an outlet for violence (a subject I later abandoned). My classmates asked me questions: "What are you trying to show?" "What do you have down already?" "Is that exactly what you mean?" I tried to respond productively. Then another classmate spoke: "That's my problem too. I know what I mean to say, but don't know how to say it." Then another, and so on. Soon, many of us were talking about our papers, trying to help one another.

Then Jeff spoke—and the class got silent. In a serious tone, he asked me, "Do you want an extension?" "Yes," I said. He gave another person who spoke up early in the discussion an extension, too. I felt like I had risked Jeff's judgement, and felt great anxiety doing so. I think the extension had the effect of punishing the other students, just because I spoke up in a moment of boldness and no one else did. Even here, when Jeff's pedagogy appeared student centered (when we ran the discussion ourselves) it had the effect of rewarding a few instead of helping everyone.

As much as Jeff might have tried to leave his power outside the class by speaking only when necessary, the students wouldn't let him. We expected him, to do things that he didn't do, such as giving strong, constructive guidance, not just critical comments. To some extent, I think my classmates and I wanted to *obey* Jeff. As my critical writing teacher said on the first day of class last week, "I know that part of acclimating yourself to a new class is trying to figure out what a professor wants." We wanted to know what Jeff wanted, but he wouldn't let us. We students had to do too much guessing.

Paradoxically, Jeff gave us nothing to obey yet forced us to obey him. This practice is not totally bad. Students need to risk our own thoughts, and some of us can do this only if we don't have the safety net of a teacher telling us what to do. Still, we need to know that our ideas will be welcomed, and since Jeff's student-centered pedagogy relied so much on his silence, we hardly had vibrant discussions of any kind in his class.

At different times, Jeff fulfilled his position of power in two ways: by being rigid—and laid back. This paradoxical approach made for some tender, shocking, and always peculiar days.

Jeff was laid back when he tried to bond with us by telling us that he had to clean up his kid's "shit" or that he played basketball with friends. When he talked about basketball, he kind of smiled. I don't know why this sort of communication didn't take place more often. One day, when we were talking about our personal experience papers, Jeff mentioned that once he found a human carcass—but then he said, "It's too early in the morning for that story." And it was, but at the time I felt like the class was together, and Jeff was just "one of us." This intimate, relaxed approach brought out the best in him. Yet, I think the class was a little suspicious of these times, for we never knew what the next day would bring. Here's an example of Jeff's strictness.

My most vivid memory of Jeff's rigidness was the day he responded to our criticisms of the class. Students were given a chance anonymously to write our biggest criticisms one Monday, and the following Wednesday Jeff responded, staunchly answering all criticisms of his teaching: "Some of you complained that I didn't come to class prepared. It took me five years to learn all of this." Then he pointed to the blackboard on which he had written all the concepts we had discussed that quarter. His responses didn't seem genuine or aimed at improving his teaching or helping the students to understand him. He thought he was always right. Jeff's position gave him responsibilities that he officially met. But he didn't take responsibility in all the ways he had led us to expect.

Jeff's rigidness and sense of correctness silenced a lot of us, and he unintentionally kept his power by maintaining silence. His own silence didn't open opportunities for us taking power, though it may have been an invitation to do just that. We can fill silence, but we didn't have a good power structure to do so. It's a nice idea for students to be self-motivated, but sometimes we aren't. Jeff tried to guide us, but his guidance was paradoxically both too formal and too informal. He wanted to follow a plan, which most teachers do, but his plan revealed itself by his simply not telling students what to do—at all.

Jeff seemed unable to respond when the look on a student's face or the silence in the classroom meant he needed to be more inviting or to explain himself more. Our subject was personal essays, yet his aloofness didn't encourage our emotions to come out. He showed us good writing, but the passion and concern for our writing seemed lacking. If we couldn't meet his ways of teaching writing, it was very difficult for him to help us produce good writing.

One thing that has become so clear to me and frightened me in writing this essay is how much I liked Jeff and how much sympathy I have for him *because* of his misguided approach. Throughout the quarter, I was almost as caught up in Jeff's ideas as he himself was. During that quarter I had horrible roommates, and Jeff's class was an escape from the chaos of my own dormitory. His rigid teaching became a spot where I (almost) knew the rules. But the rules just didn't work. Even late in the quarter, I felt like I was asking him permission for something—approval perhaps?—when I would show him my rough drafts. I was always checking with Jeff to make sure my writing and reasoning were right, and that constant, nervous checking now shows itself to me as a sign that something in Jeff's pedagogy *wasn't* right.

Since my class with Jeff, I have had several different teachers who have taken different approaches to writing instruction, approaches that have proven more beneficial than the fear of judgment I experienced in Jeff's class, which had the effect of constraining my writing. While I no longer operate under Jeff's pedagogy or his paradigms, my current studies in rhetoric and composition only make me more aware of how delicious a temptation those reductive paradigms can be. It seems so pretty and easy, the notion that we can just follow the rules and everything will work out. But it is the most destructive thing we can do to students' voices. In freshman composition—and in all writing courses—we students need to create our own identities, and only through our own voices can our own identities emerge, not by pretending foreign voices are our own. This goal may not be very easy to reach, but it's the only way to achieve growth. Students cannot fake a discourse and have it contribute to long-term writing growth, if only because faking discourse robs us of our own voices. Moreover, students know when teachers are lying. It sometimes takes us a long time—I am one example—but we do find it out. Then the unlearning of poor instruction can be difficult, but we do unlearn and relearn.

Rather than making students jump through compositional hoops, as Jeff did, teachers should from the start help students find their own voices. This can be dangerous, and is probably always difficult, but not more so than over coming another teacher's poor instruction. Despite Jeff's belief that he should vacate the class in order to bring out student voices, this paradox remains: students must have active teacher involvement at the core of any student-centered classroom. We need to be welcomed—not left to attempt masterpieces with post-high school hands. Teacher involvement is the key not only to starting conversations, but also to guiding them along their meandering paths. In Jeff's class, we were too often required to play the role of teacher. But when a teacher's "power" acts as a welcoming embrace, rather than as a vacuum, students come to develop creatively. Paradigms cannot embrace us, nor can cold confessions about how much teachers have to "help" students.

Finally, students and teachers have to get personal: students have to get into the personal to write about it, and teachers have to talk about the personal to help us talk about it. Teacher and student must work and continue conversations together because, as Paulo Freire says, "Men are not built in silence, but in word, in work, in action-reflection" (69). When we realize the classroom implications of Freire's wisdom we can overcome the isolation that often exists between teacher and students. When we recognize the necessity of mutual involvement, students and teachers can work together to achieve a pedagogy that is truly student-centered.

H. BRUCE MILLER

LIFE IS NOT MEASURED BY GRADE-POINT AVERAGES

T he New Jersey dateline on last Tuesday's story caught my eye; it's not too often that news from my old home state makes its way to this sun-washed littoral. I read a bit further and discovered that the story was about my alma mater, Princeton University. The story reported that a Princeton senior, Gabrielle Napolitano, is embroiled in a lawsuit against the university. Napolitano wrote a paper in a Spanish literature course in which she quoted extensively from a certain scholarly work. It seems that in some places Napolitano accompanied the quotations with quotation marks and footnotes and in many other places she didn't. A faculty-student committee ruled that Napolitano had committed plagiarism and that her diploma should be withheld for a year.

Napolitano, whose grade-point average is an impressive 3.7 out of a possible 4.0 and who is awaiting admission to law school, wasn't about to take that without a fight. She hired a lawyer and went to court, claiming that, in the first place, she had committed only a "technical error" rather than deliberate plagiarism and, in the second place, the punishment was out of proportion to the alleged offense. At last report a county judge had ordered the university committee to reconsider the Napolitano case, and the committee had reconsidered and reaffirmed it original decision. Whether Napolitano will appeal to the courts again is not known.

I can't attempt, on the basis of very limited knowledge of the circumstances and no knowledge at all of Napolitano, to judge the right and wrong of this case. The significant—and depressing—thing about it to me is what it seems to he saying about the place of education in modern America. Napolitano's lawsuit is just another variation on what's getting to be a common theme. Students get a lower grade in a course than they think they deserve; they sue. Students graduate and fail to get a job, or as good a job as they expected; they sue. The junior colleges and state universities have been getting hit by such litigation for years; now it looks like the plague has invaded the hitherto sacrosanct precincts of the Ivy League.

When you think about it, it's obvious that such lawsuits are a natural result of the way modern Americans look at education. We assume that the purpose of school is to provide job training, and the purpose of universities and graduate and professional schools is to provide advanced, specialized job training. The student (or the student's parents) invests a lot of money, time and work in the process; in return the educational institution is expected to deliver the goods—i.e., a degree that will provide entree to a high-paying, prestigious career. When it fails to deliver, what's more logical than to sue?

It was not always thus. Well into this century, the American university was basically either a glorified finishing-school-cum-country-club for the sons of the wealthy or a place to prepare for a career in the pulpit or the classroom, neither of which promised much in the way of what we nowadays call upward mobility. Ironically enough, Napolitano's university and mine was founded in the 1740s for the purpose of training Presbyterian clergymen. Only in the last 50 or 60 years has the American university assumed the role of springboard for socioeconomic climbers. The notion that the principal, or only, purpose of going to college is to win a ticket of admission to the great upper middle class is a fairly recent growth.

With that notion has come the frantic competitiveness, the obsession with getting into the best graduate and professional schools, the grade-grubbing—and, inevitably, the ethical corner-cutting. What seems to have all but vanished is the love of learning for its own sake, the idea that to increase one's knowledge and understanding is a worthwhile pursuit in itself.

I'd be the last one to lobby for a return to the country-club university, but it seems to me that today's college students might be happier and healthier for a little dose of some of its values. There is something terribly depressing about the thought of all those bright young people in the nation's greatest universities drudging their student years away, never lifting their eyes from the grade-point average long enough to glimpse the wonder and excitement of the intellectual world around them.

Since this is the season when the middle-aged give advice to young men and women who are leaving high school or college and are about to enter college or graduate school, here's my two cents' worth for Gabrielle Napolitano and the rest of her generation: Don't worry so much about your grades. Your life will not be permanently blighted if you get a B-plus instead of an A in Organic Chemistry 101. I can personally assure you that 15 years from now you're not going to remember the names of most of the courses you took, much less what grades you got. And don't worry so much about making money, either. You are an intelligent and capable person; you will not starve. You will not be a failure if you're not making $35,000 a year by the time you're 24. Money is overrated anyway. As William James observed, it's not lack of money but the fear of the lack of money that enslaves us.

Don't be in such a hurry to step onto the career treadmill. Don't take only the courses that you need to get into business school or that will impress the corporate recruiters. Take a few courses just because they interest you, or because they look like fun. Don't always ask, "What can I do with this?" Try asking, "What can I learn from this?" It's a beautiful and fascinating world. Enjoy it, learn about it, learn about yourself. Perhaps never again in your crowded lifetime will you have such a chance.

MALCOLM X

PRISON STUDIES

Many who today hear me somewhere in person, or on television, or those who read something I've said, will think I went to school far beyond the eighth grade. This impression is due entirely to my prison studies.

It had really begun back in the Charlestown Prison, when Bimbi first made me feel envy of his stock of knowledge. Bimbi had always taken charge of any conversation he was in, and I had tried to emulate him. But every book I picked up had few sentences which didn't contain anywhere from one to nearly all of the words that might as well have been in Chinese. When I just skipped those words, of course, I really ended up with little idea of what the book said. So I had come to the Norfolk Prison Colony still going through only book-reading motions. Pretty soon, I would have quit even these motions, unless I had received the motivation that I did.

I saw that the best thing I could do was to get hold of a dictionary—to study, to learn some words. I was lucky enough to reason also that I should try to improve my penmanship. It was sad. I couldn't even write in a straight line. It was both ideas together that made me request a dictionary along with some tablets and pencils from the Norfolk Prison Colony school.

I spent two days just riffling uncertainly through the dictionary's pages. I'd never realized so many words existed! I didn't know which words I needed to learn. Finally, to start some kind of action, I began copying.

In my slow, painstaking, ragged handwriting, I copied into my tablet everything printed on that first page, down to the punctuation marks.

I believe it took me a day. Then aloud, I read back, to myself, everything I'd written on the tablet. Over and over, aloud, to myself, I read my own handwriting.

I woke up the next morning, thinking about those words—immensely proud to realize that not only had I written so much at one time, but I'd written words that I never knew were in the world. Moreover, with a little effort, I also could remember what many of these words meant. I reviewed the words whose meanings I didn't remember. Funny thing, from the dictionary first page right now, that "aardvark" springs to my mind. The dictionary had a picture of it, a long-tailed long-eared, burrowing African mammal, which lives off termites caught by sticking out its tongue as an anteater does for ants.

I was so fascinated that I went on—I copied the dictionary's next page. And the same experience came when I studied that. With every succeeding page, I also learned of people and places and events from history. Actually the dictionary is like a miniature encyclopedia. Finally the dictionary's *A* section had filled a whole tablet—and I went on into the *B*'s. That was the way I started copying what eventually became the entire dictionary. It went a lot faster after so much practice helped me to pick up handwriting speed. Between what I wrote in my tablet, and writing letters, during the rest of my time in prison I would guess I wrote a million words.

I suppose it was inevitable that as my word-base broadened, I could for the first time pick up a book and read and now begin to understand what the book was saying. Anyone who has read a great deal can imagine the new world that opened. Let me tell you something; from then until I left that prison, in every free moment I had, if I was not reading in the library, I was reading on my bunk. You couldn't have gotten me out of books with a wedge. Between Mr. Muhammad's teachings, my correspondence, my visitors—usually Ella and Reginald—and my reading of books, months passed without my even thinking about being imprisoned. In fact, up to then, I never had been so truly free in my life . . .

As you can imagine, especially in a prison where there was heavy emphasis on rehabilitation, an inmate was smiled upon if he demonstrated an unusually intense interest in books. There was a sizable number of well-read inmates, especially the popular debaters. Some were said by many to be practically walking encyclopedias. They were almost celebrities. No university would ask any student to devour literature as I did when this new world opened to me, of being able to read and *understand*.

I read more in my room than in the library itself. An inmate who was known to read a lot could check out more than the permitted maximum number of books. I preferred reading in the total isolation of my own room.

When I had progressed to really serious reading, every night at about ten p.m. I would be outraged with the "lights out." It always seemed to catch me right in the middle of something engrossing.

Fortunately, right outside my door was a corridor light that cast a glow into my room. The glow was enough to read by, once my eyes adjusted to it. So when "lights out" came, I would sit on the floor where I could continue reading in that glow.

At one-hour intervals the night guard paced past every room. Each time I heard the approaching footsteps, I jumped into bed and feigned sleep. And as soon as the guard passed, I got back out of bed onto the floor area of that light-glow, where I would read for another fifty-eight minutes—until the guard approached again. That went on until three or four every morning. Three or four hours of sleep a night was enough for me. Often in the years in the streets I had slept less than that.

I have often reflected upon the new vistas that reading opened to me. I knew right there in prison that reading had changed forever the course of my life. As I see it today, the ability to read awoke inside me some long dormant craving to be mentally alive. I certainly wasn't seeking any degree, the way a college confers a status symbol upon its students. My homemade education gave me, with every additional book that I read, a little bit more sensitivity to the deafness, dumbness, and blindness that was afflicting the black race in America. Not long ago, an English writer telephoned me from London, asking questions. One was, "What's your alma mater?" I told him. "Books." You will never catch me with a free fifteen minutes in which I'm not studying something I feel might be able to help the black man . . .

Every time I catch a plane I have with me a book that I want to read—and that's a lot of books these days. If I weren't out here every day battling the white man, I could spend the rest of my life reading, just satisfying my curiosity—because you can hardly mention anything I'm not curious about. I don't think anybody ever got more out of going to prison than I did. In fact, prison enabled me to study far more intensively than I would have if my life had gone differently and I had attended some college. I imagine that one of the biggest troubles with colleges is there are too many distractions, too much panty-raiding, fraternities, and boola-boola and all of that. Where else but in prison could I have attacked my ignorance by being able to study intensely sometimes as much as fifteen hours a day?

bell hooks

KEEPING CLOSE TO HOME:
Class and Education

We are both awake in the almost dark of 5 A.M. Everyone else is sound asleep. Mama asks the usual questions. Telling me to look around, make sure I have everything, scolding me because I am uncertain about the actual time the bus arrives. By 5:30 we are waiting outside the closed station. Alone together, we have a chance to really talk. Mama begins. Angry with her children, especially the ones who whisper behind her back, she says bitterly, "Your childhood could not have been that bad. You were fed and clothed. You did not have to do without—that's more than a lot of folks have and I just can't stand the way y'all go on." The hurt in her voice saddens me. I have always wanted to protect mama from hurt, to ease her burdens. Now I am part of what troubles. Confronting me, she says accusingly, "It's not just the other children. You talk too much about the past. You don't just listen." And I do talk. Worse, I write about it.

Mama has always come to each of her children seeking different responses. With me she expresses the disappointment, hurt, and anger of betrayal: anger that her children are so critical, that we can't even have the sense to like the presents she sends. She says, "From now on there will be no presents. I'll just stick some money in a little envelope the way the rest of you do. Nobody wants criticism. Everybody can criticize me but I am supposed to say nothing." When I try to talk, my voice sounds like a twelve year old. When I try to talk, she speaks louder, interrupting me, even though she has said repeatedly, "Explain it to me, this talk about the past." I struggle to return to my thirty-five year old self so that she will know by the sound of my voice that we are two women talking together. It is only when I state firmly in my very adult voice, "Mama, you are not listening," that she becomes quiet. She waits. Now that I have her attention, I fear that my explanations will be lame, inadequate. "Mama," I begin, "people usually go to therapy because they feel hurt inside, because they have pain that will not stop, like a wound that continually breaks open, that does not heal. And often these hurts, that pain has to do with things that have happened in the past, sometimes in childhood, often in childhood, or things that we believe happened." She wants to know, "What hurts, what hurts are you talking about?" "Mom, I can't answer that. I can't speak for all of us, the hurts are different for everybody. But the point is you try to make the hurt better, to heal it, by understanding how it came to be. And I know you feel mad when we say something happened or hurt that you don't remember being that way, but the past isn't like that, we don't have the same memory of it. We remember things differently. You know that. And sometimes folk feel hurt about stuff and you just don't know or didn't realize it, and they need to talk about it. Surely you understand the need to talk about it."

Our conversation is interrupted by the sight of my uncle walking across the park toward us. We stop to watch him. He is on his way to work dressed in a familiar blue suit. They look alike, these two who rarely discuss the past. This interruption makes me think about life in a small town. You always see someone you know. Interruptions, intrusions are part of daily life. Privacy is difficult to maintain. We leave our private space in the car to greet him. After the hug and kiss he has given me every year since I was born, they talk about the day's funerals. In the distance the bus approaches. He walks away knowing that they will see each other later. Just before I board the bus I turn, staring into my mother's face. I am momentarily back in time, seeing myself eighteen years ago, at this same bus stop, staring into my mother's face, continually turning back, waving farewell as I returned to college—that experience which first took me away from our town, from family. Departing was as painful then as it is now. Each movement away makes return harder. Each separation intensifies distance, both physical and emotional.

To a southern black girl from a working-class background who had never been on a city bus, who had never stepped on an escalator, who had never travelled by plane, leaving the comfortable confines of a small town Kentucky life to attend Stanford University was not just frightening; it was utterly painful. My parents had not been delighted that I had been accepted and adamantly opposed my going so far from home. At the time, I did not see their opposition as an expression of their fear that they would lose me forever. Like many working-class folks, they feared what college education might do to their children's minds even as they unenthusiastically acknowledged its importance. They did not understand why I could not attend a college nearby, an all-black college. To them, any college would do. I would graduate, become a school teacher, make a decent living and a good marriage. And even though they reluctantly and skeptically supported my educational endeavors, they also subjected them to constant harsh and bitter critique. It is difficult for me to talk about my parents and their impact on me because they have always felt wary, ambivalent, mistrusting of my intellectual aspirations even as they have been caring and supportive. I want to speak about these contradictions because sorting through them, seeking resolution and reconciliation has been important to me both as it affects my development as a writer, my effort to be fully self-realized, and my longing to remain close to the family and community that provided the groundwork for much of my thinking, writing, and being.

Studying at Stanford, I began to think seriously about class differences. To be materially underprivileged at a university where most folks (with the exception of workers) are materially privileged provokes such thought. Class differences were boundaries no one wanted to face or talk about. It was easier to downplay them, to act as though we were all from privileged backgrounds, to work around them, to confront them privately in the solitude of one's room, or to pretend that just being chosen to study at such an institution meant that those of us who did not come from privilege were already in transition toward privilege. To not long for such transition marked one as rebellious, as unlikely to succeed. It was a kind of treason not to believe that it was better to be identified with the world of material privilege than with the world of the working class, the poor. No wonder our working-class parents from poor backgrounds feared our entry into such a world, intuiting perhaps that we might learn to be ashamed of where we had come from, that we might never return home, or come back only to lord it over them.

Though I hung with students who were supposedly radical and chic, we did not discuss class. I talked to no one about the sources of my shame, how it hurt me to witness the contempt shown the brown-skinned Filipina maids who cleaned our rooms, or later my concern about the $100 a month I paid for a room off-campus which was more than half of what my parents paid for rent. I talked to no one about my efforts to save money, to send a little something home. Yet these class realities separated me from fellow students. We were moving in different directions. I did not intend to forget my class background or alter my class allegiance. And even though I received an education designed to provide me with a bourgeois sensibility, passive acquiescence was not my only option. I knew that I could resist I could rebel. I could shape the direction and focus of the various forms of knowledge available to me. Even though I sometimes envied and longed for greater material advantages (particularly at vacation times when I would be one of few if any students remaining in the dormitory because there was no money for travel), I did not share the sensibility and values of my peers. That was important—class was not just about money; it was about values which showed and determined behavior. While I often needed more money, I never needed a new set of beliefs and values. For example, I was profoundly shocked and disturbed when peers would talk about their parents without respect, or would even say that they hated their parents. This was especially troubling to me when it seemed that these parents were caring and concerned. It was often explained to me that such hatred was "healthy and normal." To my white, middle-class California roommate, I explained the way we were taught to value our parents and their care, to understand that they were obligated to give us care. She would always shake her head, laughing all the while, and say, "Missy, you will learn that it's different here, that we think differently." She was right. Soon, I lived alone, like the one Mormon student who kept to himself as he made a concentrated effort to remain true to his religious beliefs and values. Later in graduate school I found that classmates believed "lower class" people had no beliefs and values. I was silent in such discussions, disgusted by their ignorance.

Carol Stack's anthropological study, *All Our Kin*, was one of the first books I read which confirmed my experiential understanding that within black culture (especially among the working class and poor, particularly in southern states), a value system emerged that was counter-hegemonic, that challenged notions of individualism and private property so important to the maintenance of white-supremacist, capitalist patriarchy. Black folk created in marginal spaces a world of community and collectivity where resources were shared. In the preface to *Feminist Theory: from margin to center*, I talked about how the point of difference, this marginality, can be the space for the formation of an oppositional world view. That world view must be articulated, named if it is to provide a sustained blueprint for change. Unfortunately, there has existed no consistent framework for such naming. Consequently both the experience of this difference and documentation of it (when it occurs) gradually loses presence and meaning.

Much of what Stack documented about the "culture of poverty," for example, would not describe interactions among most black poor today irrespective of geographical setting. Since the black people she described did not acknowledge (if they recognized it in theoretical terms) the oppositional value of their world view, apparently seeing it more as a survival strategy determined less by conscious efforts to oppose oppressive race and class biases than by circumstance, they did not attempt to establish a framework to transmit their beliefs and values from generation to generation. When circumstances changed, values altered. Efforts to assimilate the values and beliefs of privileged white people, presented through media like television, undermine and destroy potential structures of opposition.

Increasingly, young black people are encouraged by the dominant culture (and by those black people who internalize the values of this hegemony) to believe that assimilation is the only possible way to survive, to succeed. Without the framework of an organized civil rights or black resistance struggle, individual and collective efforts at black liberation that focus on the primacy of self-definition and self-determination often go unrecognized. It is crucial that those among us who resist and rebel, who survive and succeed, speak openly and honestly about our lives and the nature of our personal struggles, the means by which we resolve and reconcile contradictions. This is no easy task. Within the educational institutions where we learn to develop and strengthen our writing and analytical skills, we also learn to think, write, and talk in a manner that shifts attention away from personal experience. Yet if we are to reach our people and all people, if we are to remain connected (especially those of us whose familial backgrounds are poor and working class), we must understand that the telling of one's personal story provides a meaningful example, a way for folks to identify and connect.

Combining personal with critical analysis and theoretical perspectives can engage listeners who might otherwise feel estranged, alienated. To speak simply with language that is accessible to as many folks as possible is also important. Speaking about one's personal experience or speaking with simple language is often considered by academics and/or intellectuals (irrespective of their political inclinations) to be a sign of intellectual weakness or even anti-intellectualism. Lately, when I speak, I do not stand in place—reading my paper, making little or no eye contact with audiences—but instead make eye contact, talk extemporaneously, digress, and address the audience directly. I have been told that people assume I am not prepared, that I am anti-intellectual, unprofessional (a concept that has everything to do with class as it determines actions and behavior), or that I am reinforcing the stereotype of black as non-theoretical and gutsy.

Such criticism was raised recently by fellow feminist scholars after a talk I gave at Northwestern University at a conference on "Gender, Culture, Politics" to an audience that was mainly students and academics. I deliberately chose to speak in a very basic way, thinking especially about the few community folks who had come to hear me. Weeks later, KumKum Sangari, a fellow participant who shared with me what was said when I was no longer present, and I engaged in quite rigorous critical dialogue about the way my presentation had been perceived primarily by privileged white female academics. She was concerned that I not mask my knowledge of theory, that I not appear anti-intellectual. Her critique compelled me to articulate concerns that I am often silent about with colleagues. I spoke about class allegiance and revolutionary commitments, explaining that it was disturbing to me that intellectual radicals who speak about transforming society, ending the domination of race, sex, class, cannot break with behavior patterns that reinforce and perpetuate domination, or continue to use as their sole reference point how we might be or are perceived by those who dominate, whether or not we gain their acceptance and approval.

This is a primary contradiction which raises the issue of whether or not the academic setting is a place where one can be truly radical or subversive. Concurrently, the use of a language and style of presentation that alienates most folks who are not also academically trained reinforces the notion that the academic world is separate from real life, that everyday world where we constantly adjust our language and behavior to meet diverse needs. The academic setting is separate only when we work to make it so. It is a false dichotomy which suggests that academics and/or intellectuals can only speak to one another, that we cannot hope to speak with the masses. What is true is that we make choices, that we choose our audiences, that we choose voices to hear and voices to silence. If I do not speak in a language that can be understood, then there is little chance for dialogue. This issue of language and behavior is a central contradiction all radical intellectuals, particularly those who are members of oppressed groups, must continually confront and work to resolve. One of the clear and present dangers that exists when we move outside our class of origin, our collective ethnic experience, and enter hierarchical institutions which daily reinforce domination by race, sex, and class, is that we gradually assume a mindset similar to those who dominate and oppress, that we lose critical consciousness because it is not reinforced or affirmed by the environment. We must be ever vigilant. It is important that we know who we are speaking to, who we most want to hear us, who we most long to move, motivate, and touch with our words.

When I first came to New Haven to teach at Yale, I was truly surprised by the marked class divisions between black folks—students and professors—who identify with Yale and those black folks who work at Yale or in surrounding communities. Style of dress and self-presentation are most often the central markers of one's position. I soon learned that the black folks who spoke on the street were likely to be part of the black community and those who carefully shifted their glance were likely to be associated with Yale. Walking with a black female colleague one day, I spoke to practically every black person in sight (a gesture which reflects my upbringing), an action which disturbed my companion. Since I addressed black folk who were clearly not associated with Yale, she wanted to know whether or not I knew them. That was funny to me. "Of course not," I answered. Yet when I thought about it seriously, I realized that in a deep way, I knew them for they, and not my companion or most of my colleagues at Yale, resemble my family. Later that year, in a black women's support group I started for undergraduates, students from poor backgrounds spoke about the shame they sometimes feel when faced with the reality of their connection to working-class and poor black people. One student confessed that her father is a street person, addicted to drugs, someone who begs from passersby. She, like other Yale students, turns away from street people often, sometimes showing anger or contempt; she hasn't wanted anyone to know that she was related to this kind of person. She struggles with this, wanting to find a way to acknowledge and affirm this reality, to claim this connection. The group asked me and one another what we [should] do to remain connected, to honor the bonds we have with working-class and poor people even as our class experience alters.

Maintaining connections with family and community across class boundaries demands more than just summary recall of where one's roots are, where one comes from. It requires knowing, naming, and being ever-mindful of those aspects of one's past that have enabled and do enable one's self-development in the present, that sustain and support, that enrich. One must also honestly confront barriers that do exist, aspects of that past that do diminish. My parents' ambivalence about my love for reading led to intense conflict. They (especially my mother) would work to ensure that I had access to books, but would threaten to burn the books or throw them away if I did not conform to other expectations. Or they would insist that reading too much would drive me insane. Their ambivalence nurtured in me a like uncertainty about the value and significance of intellectual endeavor which took years for me to unlearn. While this aspect of our class reality was one that wounded and diminished, their vigilant insistence that being smart did not make me a "better" or "superior" person (which often got on my nerves because I think I wanted to have that sense that it did indeed set me apart, make me better) made a profound impression. From them I learned to value and respect various skills and talents folk might have, not just to value people who read books and talk about ideas. They and my grandparents might say about somebody, "Now he don't read nor write a lick, but he can tell a story," or as my grandmother would say, "call out the hell in words."

Empty romanticization of poor or working-class backgrounds undermines the possibility of true connection. Such connection is based on understanding difference in experience and perspective and working to mediate and negotiate these terrains. Language is a crucial issue for folk whose movement outside the boundaries of poor and working-class backgrounds changes the nature and direction of their speech. Coming to Stanford with my own version of a Kentucky accent, which I think of always as a strong sound quite different from Tennessee or Georgia speech, I learned to speak differently while maintaining the speech of my region, the sound of my family and community. This was of course much easier to keep up when I returned home to stay often. In recent years, I have endeavored to use various speaking styles in the classroom as a teacher and find it disconcerts those who feel that the use of a particular patois excludes them as listeners, even if there is translation into the usual, acceptable mode of speech. Learning to listen to different voices, hearing different speech challenges the notion that we must all assimilate—share a single, similar talk—in educational institutions. Language reflects the culture from which we emerge. To deny ourselves daily use of speech patterns that are common and familiar, that embody the unique and distinctive aspect of our self is one of the ways we become estranged and alienated from our past. It is important for us to have as many languages on hand as we can know or learn. It is important for those of us who are black, who speak in particular patois as well as standard English, to express ourselves in both ways.

Often I tell students from poor and working-class backgrounds that if you believe what you have learned and are learning in schools and universities separates you from your past, this is precisely what will happen. It is important to stand firm in the conviction that nothing can truly separate us from our pasts when we nurture and cherish that connection. An important strategy for maintaining contact is ongoing acknowledgment of the primacy of one's past, of one's background, affirming the reality that such bonds are not severed automatically solely because one enters a new environment or moves toward a different class experience.

Again, I do not wish to romanticize this effort, to dismiss the reality of conflict and contradiction. During my time at Stanford, I did go through a period of more than a year when I did not return home. That period was one where I felt that it was simply too difficult to mesh my profoundly disparate realities. Critical reflection about the choice I was making, particularly about why I felt a choice had to be made, pulled me through this difficult time. Luckily I recognized that the insistence on choosing between the world of family and community and the new world of privileged white people and privileged ways of knowing was imposed upon me by the outside. It is as though a mythical contract had been signed somewhere which demanded of us black folks that once we entered these spheres we would immediately give up all vestiges of our underprivileged past. It was my responsibility to formulate a way of being that would allow me to participate fully in my new environment while integrating and maintaining aspects of the old.

One of the most tragic manifestations of the pressure black people feel to assimilate is expressed in the internalization of racist perspectives. I was shocked and saddened when I first heard black professors at Stanford downgrade and express contempt for black students, expecting us to do poorly, refusing to establish nurturing bonds. At every university I have attended as a student or worked at as a teacher, I have heard similar attitudes expressed with little or no understanding of factors that might prevent brilliant black students from performing to their full capability. Within universities, there are few educational and social spaces where students who wish to affirm positive ties to ethnicity—to blackness, to working-class backgrounds—can receive affirmation and support. Ideologically, the message is clear—assimilation is the way to gain acceptance and approval from those in power.

Many white people enthusiastically supported Richard Rodriguez's vehement contention in his autobiography, *Hunger of Memory*, that attempts to maintain ties with his Chicano background impeded his progress, that he had to sever ties with community and kin to succeed at Stanford and in the larger world, that family language, in his case Spanish, had to be made secondary or discarded. If the terms of success as defined by the standards of ruling groups within white-supremacist, capitalist patriarchy are the only standards that exist, then assimilation is indeed necessary. But they are not. Even in the face of powerful structures of domination, it remains possible for each of us, especially those of us who are members of oppressed and/or exploited groups as well as those radical visionaries who may have race, class, and sex privilege, to define and determine alternative standards, to decide on the nature and extent of compromise. Standards by which one's success is measured, whether student or professor, are quite different from those of us who wish to resist reinforcing the domination of race, sex, and class, who work to maintain and strengthen our ties with the oppressed, with those who lack material privilege, with our families who are poor and working-class.

When I wrote my first book, *Ain't I a Woman: black women and feminism*, the issue of class and its relationship to who one's reading audience might be came up for me around my decision not to use footnotes, for which I have been sharply criticized. I told people that my concern was that footnotes set class boundaries for readers, determining who a book is for. I was shocked that many academic folks scoffed at this idea. I shared that I went into working-class black communities as well as talked with family and friends to survey whether or not they ever read books with footnotes and found that they did not. A few did not know what they were, but most folks saw them as indicating that a book was for college-educated people. These responses influenced my decision. When some of my more radical, college-educated friends freaked out about the absence of footnotes, I seriously questioned how we could ever imagine revolutionary transformation of society if such a small shift in direction could be viewed as threatening. Of course, many folks warned that the absence of footnotes would make the work less credible in academic circles. This information also highlighted the way in which class informs our choices. Certainly I did feel that choosing to use simple language, absence of footnotes, etc. would mean I was jeopardizing the possibility of being taken seriously in academic circles but then this was a political matter and a political decision. It utterly delights me that this has proven not to be the case and that the book is read by many academics as well as people who are not college-educated.

Always our first response when we are motivated to conform or compromise within structures that reinforce domination must be to engage in critical reflection. Only by challenging ourselves to push against oppressive boundaries do we make the radical alternative possible, expanding the realm and scope of critical inquiry. Unless we share radical strategies, ways of rethinking and revisioning with students, with kin and community. With a larger audience, we risk perpetuating the stereotype that we succeed because we are the exception, different from the rest of our people. Since I left home and entered college, I am often asked, usually by white people, if my sisters and brothers are also high achievers. At the root of this question is the longing for reinforcement of the belief in "the exception" which enables race, sex, and class biases to remain intact. I am careful to separate what it means to be exceptional from a notion of "the exception."

Frequently I hear smart black folks, from poor and working-class backgrounds, stressing their frustration that at times family and community do not recognize that they are exceptional. Absence of positive affirmation clearly diminishes the longing to excel in academic endeavors. Yet it is important to distinguish between the absence of basic positive affirmation and the longing for continued reinforcement that we are special. Usually liberal white folks will willingly offer continual reinforcement of us as exceptions—as special. This can be both patronizing and very seductive.

Since we often work in situations where we are isolated from other black folks, we can easily begin to feel that encouragement from white people is the primary or only source of support and recognition. Given the internalization of racism, it is easy to view this support as more validating and legitimizing than similar support from black people. Still, nothing takes the place of being valued and appreciated by one's own, by one's family and community. We share a mutual and reciprocal responsibility for affirming one another's successes. Sometimes we have to talk to our folks about the fact that we need their ongoing support and affirmation, that it is unique and special to us. In some cases we may never receive desired recognition and acknowledgment of specific achievements from kin. Rather than seeing this as a basis for estrangement, for severing connection, it is useful to explore other sources of nourishment and support.

I do not know that my mother's mother ever acknowledged my college education except to ask me once, "How can you live so far away from your people?" Yet she gave me sources of affirmation and nourishment, sharing the legacy her quilt-making, of family history, of her incredible way with words. Recently, when our father retired after more than thirty years of work as a janitor, I wanted to pay tribute to this experience, to identify links between his work and my own as writer and teacher. Reflecting on our family I recalled ways he had been an impressive example of diligence and hard work approaching tasks with a seriousness of concentration I work to mirror and develop, with a discipline I struggle to maintain. Sharing these thoughts with him keeps us connected, nurtures our respect for each other, maintaining a space, however large or small, where we can talk.

Open, honest communication is the most important way we maintain relationships with kin and community as our class experience and backgrounds change. It is as vital as the sharing of resources. Often financial assistance is given in circumstances where there is no meaningful contact. However helpful, this can also be an expression of estrangement and alienation. Communication between black folks from various experiences of material privilege was much easier when we were all in segregated communities sharing common experiences in relation to social institutions. Without this grounding, we must work to maintain ties, connection. We must assume greater responsibility for making and maintaining contact, connections that can shape our intellectual visions and inform our radical commitments. The most powerful resource any of us can have as we study and teach in university settings is full understanding and appreciation of the richness, beauty, and primacy of our familial and community backgrounds. Maintaining awareness of class differences, nurturing ties with the poor and working-class people who are our most intimate kin, our comrades in struggle, transforms and enriches our intellectual experience. Education as the practice of freedom becomes not a force which fragments or separates, but one that brings us closer, expanding our definitions of home and community.

EARL SHORRIS

ON THE USES OF A
LIBERAL EDUCATION
AS A WEAPON IN THE
HANDS OF THE
RESTLESS POOR

Next month I will publish a book about poverty in America, but not the book I intended. The world took me by surprise—not once, but again and again. The poor themselves led me in directions I could not have imagined, especially the one that came out of a conversation in a maximum-security prison for women that is set, incongruously, in a lush Westchester suburb fifty miles north of New York City.

I had been working on the book for about three years when I went to the Bedford Hills Correctional Facility for the first time. The staff and inmates had developed a program to deal with family violence, and I wanted to see how their ideas fit with what I had learned about poverty.

Numerous forces—hunger, isolation, illness, landlords, police, abuse, neighbors, drugs, criminals, and racism, among many others—exert themselves on the poor at all times and enclose them, making up a "surround of force" from which, it seems, they cannot escape. I had come to understand that this was what kept the poor from being political and that the absence of politics in their lives was what kept them poor. I don't mean "political" in the sense of voting in an election but in the way Thucydides used the word: to mean activity with other people at every level, from the family to the neighborhood to the broader community to the city-state.

By the time I got to Bedford Hills, I had listened to more than six hundred people, some of them over the course of two or three years. Although my method is that of the *bricoleur*, the tinkerer who assembles a thesis of the bric-a-brac he finds in the world, I did not think there would be any more surprises. But I had not counted on what Viniece Walker was to say.

It is considered bad form in prison to speak of a person's crime, and I will follow that precise etiquette here. I can tell you that Viniece Walker came to Bedford Hills when she was twenty years old, a high school dropout who read at the level of a college sophomore, a graduate of crackhouses, the streets of Harlem, and a long alliance with a brutal man. On the surface Viniece has remained as tough as she was on the street. She speaks bluntly, and even though she is HIV positive and the virus has progressed during her time in prison, she still swaggers as she walks down the long prison corridors. While in prison, Niecie, as she is known to her friends, completed her high school requirements and began to pursue a college degree (psychology is the only major offered at Bedford Hills, but Niecie also took a special interest in philosophy). She became a counselor to women with a history of family violence and a comforter to those with AIDS.

Only the deaths of other women cause her to stumble in the midst of her swaggering step, to spend days alone with the remorse that drives her to seek redemption. She goes through life as if she had been imagined by Dostoevsky, but even more complex than his fictions, alive, a person, a fair-skinned and freckled African-American woman, and in prison. It was she who responded to my sudden question, "Why do you think people are poor?"

We had never met before. The conversation around us focused on the abuse of women. Niecie's eyes were perfectly opaque—hostile, prison eyes. Her mouth was set in the beginning of a sneer.

"You got to begin with the children," she said, speaking rapidly, clipping out the street sounds as they came into her speech.

She paused long enough to let the change of direction take effect, then resumed the rapid, rhythmless speech "You've got to teach the moral life of downtown to the children. And the way you do that, Earl, is by taking them downtown to plays, museums, concerts, lectures, where they can learn the moral life of downtown."

I smiled at her, misunderstanding, thinking I was indulging her. "And then they won't be poor anymore?"

She read every nuance of my response, and answered angrily, "And they won't be poor no more."

"What you mean is—"

"What I mean is what I said—a moral alternative to the street."

She didn't speak of jobs or money. In that, she was like the others I had listened to. No one had spoken of jobs or money. But how could the "moral life of downtown" lead anyone out from the surround of force? How could a museum push poverty away? Who can dress in statues or eat the past? And what of the political life? Had Niecie skipped a step or failed to take a step? The way out of poverty was politics, not the "moral life of down-town." But to enter the public world, to practice the political life, the poor had first to learn to reflect. That was what Niecie meant by the "moral life of downtown." She did not make the error of divorcing ethics from politics. Niecie had simply said, in a kind of shorthand, that no one could step out of the panicking circumstance of poverty directly into the public world.

Although she did not say so, I was sure that when she spoke of the "moral life of downtown" she meant something that had happened to her. With no job and no money, a prisoner, she had undergone a radical trans-formation. She had followed the same path that led to the invention of politics in ancient Greece. She had learned to reflect. In further conversa-tion it became clear that when she spoke of "the moral life of downtown" she meant the humanities, the study of human constructs and concerns, which has been the source of reflection for the secular world since the Greeks first stepped back from nature to experience wonder at what they beheld. If the political life was the way out of poverty, the humanities pro-vided an entrance to reflection and the political life. The poor did not need anyone to release them; an escape route existed. But to open this avenue to reflection and politics a major distinction between the preparation for the life of the rich and the life of the poor had to be eliminated.

Once Niecie had challenged me with her theory, the comforts of tinkering came to an end; I could no longer make an homage to the happenstance world and rest. To test Niecie's theory, students, faculty, and facilities were required. Quantitative measures would have to be developed; anecdotal information would also be useful. And the ethics of the experiment had to be considered: I resolved to do no harm. There was no need for the course to have a "sink or swim" character; it could aim to keep as many afloat as possible.

When the idea for an experimental course became clear in my mind, I discussed it with Dr. Jaime Inclan, director of the Roberto Clemente Family Guidance Center in lower Manhattan, a facility that provides counseling to poor people, mainly Latinos, in their own language and in their own community. Dr. Inclan offered the center's conference room for a classroom. We would put three metal tables end-to-end to approximate the boat-shaped tables used in discussion sections at the University of Chicago of the Hutchins era,[1] which I used as a model for the course. A card table in the back of the room would hold a coffeemaker and a few cookies. The setting was not elegant, but it would do. And the front wall was covered by a floor-to-ceiling blackboard.

Now the course lacked only students and teachers. With no funds and a budget that grew every time a new idea for the course crossed my mind, I would have to ask the faculty to donate its time and effort. Moreover, when Hutchins said, "The best education for the best is the best education for us all," he meant it: he insisted that full professors teach discussion sections in the college. If the Clemente Course in the Humanities was to follow the same pattern, it would require a faculty with the knowledge and prestige that students might encounter in their first year at Harvard, Yale, Princeton, or Chicago.

---

1. Under the guidance of Robert Maynard Hutchins (1929-1951), the University of Chicago required year-long courses in the humanities, social sciences, and natural sciences for the Bachelor of Arts degree. Hutchins developed the curriculum with the help of Mortimer Adler, among others; the Hutchins courses later influenced Adler's Great Books program.

I turned first to the novelist Charles Simmons. He had been assistant editor of *The New York Times Book Review* and had taught at Columbia University. He volunteered to teach poetry, beginning with simple poems, Housman, and ending with Latin poetry. Grace Glueck, who writes art news and criticism for the *New York Times*, planned a course that began with cave paintings, and ended in the late twentieth century. Timothy Koranda, who did his graduate work at MIT, had published journal articles on mathematical logic, but he had been away from his field for some years and looked forward to getting back to it. I planned to teach the American history course through documents, beginning with the Magna Carta, moving on to the second of Locke's *Two Treatises of Government*, the Declaration of Independence, and so on through the documents of the Civil War. I would also teach the political philosophy class.

Since I was a naïf in this endeavor, it did not immediately occur to me that recruiting students would present a problem. I didn't know how many I needed. All I had were criteria for selection:

Age: 18-35.

Household income: Less than 150 percent of the Census Bureau's Official Poverty Threshold (though this was to change slightly).

Educational level: Ability to read a tabloid newspaper.

Educational goals: An expression of intent to complete the course.

Dr. Inclan arranged a meeting of community activists who could help recruit students. Lynette Lauretig of The Door, a program that provides medical and educational services to adolescents, and Angel Roman of the Grand Street Settlement, which offers work and training and GED programs, were both willing to give us access to prospective students. They also pointed out some practical considerations. The course had to provide bus and subway tokens, because fares ranged between three and six dollars per class per student, and the students could not afford sixty or even thirty dollars a month for transportation. We also had to offer dinner or a snack, because the classes were to be held from 6:00 to 7:30 P.M.

The first recruiting session came only a few days later. Nancy Mamis-King, associate executive director of the Neighborhood Youth & Family Services program in the South Bronx, had identified some Clemente Course candidates and had assembled about twenty of her clients and their supervisors in a circle of chairs in a conference room. Everyone in the room was black or Latino, with the exception of one social worker and me.

After I explained the idea of the course, the white social worker was the first to ask a question: "Are you going to teach African history?"

"No. We'll be teaching a section on American history, based on documents, as I said. We want to teach the ideas of history so that—"

"You have to teach African history."

"This is America, so we'll teach American history. If we were in Africa, I would teach African history, and if we were in China, I would teach Chinese history."

"You're indoctrinating people in Western culture."

I tried to get beyond her, "We'll study African art," I said, "as it affects art in America. We'll study American history and literature; you can't do that without studying African-American culture, because culturally all Americans are black as well as white, Native American, Asian, and so on." It was no use; not one of them applied for admission to the course.

A few days later Lynette Lauretig arranged a meeting with some of her staff at The Door. We disagreed about the course. They thought it should be taught at a much lower level. Although I could not change their views, they agreed to assemble a group of Door members who might be interested in the humanities.

On an early evening that same week, about twenty prospective students were scheduled to meet in a classroom at The Door. Most of them came late. Those who arrived first slumped in their chairs, staring at the floor or greeting me with sullen glances. A few ate candy or what appeared to be the remnants of a meal. The students were mostly black and Latino, one was Asian, and five were white; two of the whites were immigrants who had severe problems with English. When I introduced myself, several of the students would not shake my hand, two or three refused even to look at me, one girl giggled, and the last person to volunteer his name, a young man dressed in a Tommy Hilfiger sweatshirt and wearing a cap turned sideways, drawled, "Henry Jones, but they call me Sleepy, because I got these sleepy eyes—"

"In our class, we'll call you Mr. Jones."

He smiled and slid down in his chair so that his back was parallel to the floor.

Before I finished attempting to shake hands with the prospective students, a waiflike Asian girl with her mouth half-full of cake said, "Can we get on with it? I'm bored."

 I liked the group immediately.

Having failed in the South Bronx, I resolved to approach these prospective students differently. "You've been cheated," I said. "Rich people learn the humanities; you didn't. The humanities are a foundation for getting along in the world, for thinking, for learning to reflect on the world instead of just reacting to whatever force is turned against you. I think the humanities are one of the ways to become political, and I don't mean political in the sense of voting in an election but in the broad sense." I told them Thucydides' definition of politics.

"Rich people know politics in that sense. They know how to negotiate instead of using force. They know how to use politics to get along, to get power. It doesn't mean that rich people are good and poor people are bad. It simply means that rich people know a more effective method for living in this society.

"Do all rich people, or people who are in the middle, know the humanities? Not a chance. But some do. And it helps. It helps to live better and enjoy life more. Will the humanities make you rich? Yes. Absolutely. But not in terms of money. In terms of life.

"Rich people learn the humanities in private schools and expensive universities. And that's one of the ways in which they learn the political life. I think that is the real difference between the haves and have-nots in this country. If you want real power, legitimate power, the kind that comes from the people and belongs to the people, you must understand politics. The humanities will help.

"Here's how it works: We'll pay your subway fare; take care of your children, if you have them; give you a snack or a sandwich; provide you with books and any other materials you need. But we'll make you think harder, use your mind more fully, than you ever have before. You'll have to read and think about the same kinds of ideas you would encounter in a first-year course at Harvard or Yale or Oxford.

"You'll have to come to class in the snow and the rain and the cold and the dark. No one will coddle you; no one will slow down for you. There will be tests to take, papers to write. And I can't promise you anything but a certificate of completion at the end of the course. I'll be talking to colleges about giving credit for the course, but I can't promise anything. If you come to the Clemente Course, you must do it because you want to study the humanities, because you want a certain kind of life, a richness of mind and spirit. That's all I offer you: philosophy, poetry, art history, logic, rhetoric, and American history."

"Your teachers will all be people of accomplishment in their fields," I said, and I spoke a little about each teacher. "That's the course. October through May, with a two-week break at Christmas. It is generally accepted in America that the liberal arts and the humanities in particular belong to the elites. I think you're the elites."

The young Asian woman said, "What are you getting out of this?"

"This is a demonstration project. I'm writing a book. This will be proof, I hope, of my idea about the humanities. Whether it succeeds or fails will be up to the teachers and you."

All but one of the prospective students applied for admission to the course.

I repeated the new presentation at the Grand Street Settlement and at other places around the city. There were about fifty candidates for the thirty positions in the course. Personal interviews began in early September.

Meanwhile, almost all of my attempts to raise money had failed. Only the novelist Starling Lawrence, who is also editor in chief of W. W. Norton, which had contracted to publish the book; the publishing house itself; and a small, private family foundation supported the experiment. We were far short of our budgeted expenses, but my wife, Sylvia, and I agreed that the cost was still very low, and we decided to go ahead.

Of the fifty prospective students who showed up at the Clemente Center for personal interviews, a few were too rich (a postal supervisor's son, a fellow who claimed his father owned a factory in Nigeria that employed sixty people), and more than a few could not read. Two home-care workers from Local 1199 could not arrange their hours to enable them to take the course. Some of the applicants were too young: a thirteen-year-old and two who had just turned sixteen.

Lucia Medina, a woman with five children who told me that she often answered the door at the single-room occupancy hotel where she lived with a butcher knife in her hand, was the oldest person accepted into the course. Carmen Quiñones, a recovering addict who had spent time in prison, was the next eldest. Both were in their early thirties.

The interviews went on for days.

Abel Lomas[2] shared an apartment and worked part-time wrapping packages at Macy's. His father had abandoned the family when Abel was born. His mother was murdered by his stepfather when Abel was thirteen. With no one to turn to and no place to stay, he lived on the streets, first in Florida, then back in New York City. He used the tiny stipend from his mother's Social Security to keep himself alive.

After the recruiting session at The Door, I drove up Sixth Avenue from Canal Street with Abel, and we talked about ethics. He had a street tough's delivery, spitting out his ideas in crudely formed sentences of four, five, eight words, strings of blunt declarations, with never a dependent clause to qualify his thoughts. He did not clear his throat with badinage, as timidity teaches us to do, nor did he waste his breath with tact.

"What do you think about drugs?" he asked, the strangely breathless delivery further coarsened by his Dominican accent. "My cousin is a dealer."

"I've seen a lot of people hurt by drugs."

"Your family has nothing to eat. You sell drugs. What's worse? Let your family starve or sell drugs?'

"Starvation and drug addiction are both bad, aren't they?"

"Yes," he said, not "yeah" or "uh-huh" but a precise, almost formal yes."

"So it's a question of the worse of two evils? How shall we decide?"

The question came up near Thirty-fourth Street, where Sixth Avenue remains hellishly traffic-jammed well into the night. Horns honked, people flooded into the streets against the light. Buses and trucks and taxicabs

---

2. Not his real name.

threatened their way from one lane to the next where the overcrowded avenue crosses the equally crowded Broadway. As we passed Herald Square and made our way north again, I said, "There are a couple of ways to look at it. One comes from Immanuel Kant, who said that you should not do anything unless you want it to become a universal law, that is, unless you think it's what everybody should do. So Kant wouldn't agree to selling drugs or letting your family starve."

Again he answered with a formal "Yes."

"There's another way to look at it, which is to ask what is the greatest good for the greatest number: in this case, keeping your family from starvation or keeping tens, perhaps hundreds of people from losing their lives to drugs. So which is the greatest good for the greatest number?"

"That's what I think," he said.

"What?"

"You shouldn't sell drugs. You can always get food to eat. Welfare. Something."

"You're a Kantian."

"Yes."

"You know who Kant is?"

"I think so."

We had arrived at Seventy-seventh Street, where he got out of the car to catch the subway before I turned east. As he opened the car door and the light came on, the almost military neatness of him struck me. He had the newly cropped hair of a cadet. His clothes were clean, without a wrinkle. He was an orphan, a street kid, an immaculate urchin. Within a few weeks he would be nineteen years old, the Social Security payments would end, and he would have to move into a shelter.

Some of those who came for interviews were too poor. I did not think that was possible when we began, and I would like not to believe it now, but it was true. There is a point at which the level of forces that surround the poor can become insurmountable, when there is no time or energy left to be anything but poor. Most often I could not recruit such people for the course; when I did, they soon dropped out.

Over the days of interviewing, a class slowly assembled. I could not then imagine who would last the year and who would not. One young woman submitted a neatly typed essay that said, "I was homeless once, then I lived for some time in a shelter. Right now, I have got my own space granted by the Partnership for the Homeless. Right now, I am living alone, with very limited means. Financially I am overwhelmed by debts. I cannot afford all the food I need . . ."

A brother and sister, refugees from Tashkent, lived with their parents in the farthest reaches of Queens, far beyond the end of the subway line. They had no money, and they had been refused admission by every school to which they had applied. I had not intended to accept immigrants or people who had difficulty with the English language, but I took them into the class.

I also took four who had been in prison, three who were homeless, three who were pregnant, one who lived in a drugged dream-state in which she was abused, and one whom I had known for a long time and who was dying of AIDS. As I listened to them, I wondered how the course would affect them. They had no public life, no place; they lived within the surround of force, moving as fast as they could, driven by necessity, without a moment to reflect. Why should they care about fourteenth century Italian painting or truth tables or the death of Socrates?

Between the end of recruiting and the orientation session that would open the course, I made a visit to Bedford Hills to talk with Niecie Walker. It was hot, and the drive up from the city had been unpleasant. I didn't yet know Niecie very well. She didn't trust me, and I didn't know what to make of her. While we talked, she held a huge white pill in her hand. "For AIDS," she said.

"Are you sick?"

"My T-cell count is down. But that's neither here nor there. Tell me about the course, Earl. What are you going to teach?"

"Moral philosophy."

"And what does that include?"

She had turned the visit into an interrogation. I didn't mind. At the end of the conversation I would be going out into "the free world"; if she wanted our meeting to be an interrogation, I was not about to argue. I said, "We'll begin with Plato: the *Apology*, a little of the *Crito*, a few pages of the *Phaedo* so that they'll know what happened to Socrates. Then we'll read Aristotle's *Nicomachean Ethics*. I also want them to read Thucydides, particularly Pericles' Funeral Oration in order to make the connection between ethics and politics, to lead then in the direction I hope the course will take them. Then we'll end with *Antigone*, but read as moral and political philosophy as well as drama."

"There's something missing," she said, leaning back in her chair, taking on an air of superiority.

The drive had been long, the day was hot, the air in the room was dead and damp. "Oh, yeah," I said, "and what's that?"

"Plato's Allegory of the Cave. How can you teach philosophy to poor people without the Allegory of the Cave? The ghetto is the cave. Education is the light. Poor people can understand that."

At the beginning of the orientation at the Clemente Center a week later, each teacher spoke for a minute or two. Dr. Inclan and his research assistant, Patricia Vargas, administered the questionnaire he had devised to measure, as best he could, the role of force and the amount of reflection in the lives of the students. I explained that each class was going to be videotaped as another way of documenting the project. Then I gave out the first assignment: "In preparation for our next meeting, I would like you to read a brief selection from Plato's *Republic*: the Allegory of the Cave."

I tried to guess how many students would return for the first class. I hoped for twenty, expected fifteen, and feared ten. Sylvia, who had agreed to share the administrative tasks of the course, and I prepared coffee and cookies for twenty-five. We had a plastic container filled with subway tokens. Thanks to Starling Lawrence, we had thirty copies of Bernard Knox's *Norton Book of Classical Literature*, which contained all of the texts for the philosophy section except the *Republic* and the *Nicomachean Ethics*.

At six o'clock there were only ten students seated around the long table, but by six-fifteen the number had doubled, and a few minutes later two more straggled in out of the dusk. I had written a time line on the blackboard, showing them the temporal progress of thinking—from the role of myth in Neolithic societies to *The Gilgamesh Epic* and forward to the Old Testament, Confucius, the Greeks, the New Testament, the Koran, the *Epic of Son-Jara*, and ending with Nahuatl and Maya poems, which took us up to the contact between Europe and America, where the history course began. The time line served as context and geography as well as history: no race, no major culture was ignored. "Let's agree," I told them, "that we are all human, whatever our origins. And now let's go into Plato's cave."

I told them that there would be no lectures in the philosophy section of the course; we would use the Socratic method, which is called maieutic dialogue. "'Maieutic' comes from the Greek word for midwifery. I'll take the role of midwife in our dialogue. Now, what do you mean by that? What does a midwife do?"

It was the beginning of a love affair, the first moment of their infatuation with Socrates. Later, Abel Lomas would characterize that moment in his no-nonsense fashion, saying that it was the first time anyone had ever paid attention to their opinions.

Grace Glueck began the art history class in a darkened room lit with slides of the Lascaux caves and next turned the students' attention to Egypt, arranging for them to visit the Metropolitan Museum of Art to see the Temple of Dendur and the Egyptian Galleries. They arrived at the museum on a Friday evening. Darlene Codd brought her two-year-old son. Pearl Lau was late, as usual. One of the students, who had told me how much he was looking forward to the museum visit, didn't show up, which surprised me. Later I learned that he had been arrested for jumping a turnstile in a subway station on his way to the museum and was being held in a prison cell under the Brooklyn criminal courthouse. In the Temple of Dendur, Samantha Smoot asked questions of Felicia Blum, a museum lecturer. Samantha was the student who had burst out with the news, in one of the first sessions of the course, that people in her neighborhood believed it "wasn't no use goin' to school, because the white man wouldn't let you up no matter what." But in a hall where the statuary was of half-human, half-animal female figures, it was Samantha who asked what the glyphs meant, encouraging Felicia Blum to read them aloud, to translate them into English. Toward the end of the evening, Grace led the students out of the halls of antiquities into the Rockefeller Wing, where she told them of the collections of culture and art in Mali, Benin, and the Pacific Islands. When the students had collected their coats and stood together near the entrance to the museum, preparing to leave, Samantha stood apart, a tall, slim young woman, dressed in a deerstalker cap and a dark blue peacoat. She made an exaggerated farewell wave at us and returned to Egypt—her ancient mirror.

Charles Simmons began the poetry class with poems as puzzles and laughs. His plan was to surprise the class, and he did. At first he read the poems aloud to them, interrupting himself with footnotes to bring them along. He showed them poems of love and of seduction, and satiric commentaries on those poems by later poets. "Let us read," the students demanded, but Charles refused. He tantalized them with the opportunity to read poems aloud. A tug-of-war began between him and the students, and the standoff was ended not by Charles directly but by Hector Anderson. When Charles asked if anyone in the class wrote poetry, Hector raised his hand.

"Can you recite one of your poems for us?" Charles said.

Until that moment, Hector had never volunteered a comment, though he had spoken well and intelligently when asked. He preferred to slouch in his chair, dressed in full camouflage gear, wearing a nylon stocking over his hair and eating slices of fresh cantaloupe or honeydew melon.

In response to Charles's question, Hector slid up to a sitting position. "If you turn that camera off," he said. "I don't want anybody using my lyrics." When he was sure the red light of the video camera was off, Hector stood and recited verse after verse of a poem that belonged somewhere in the triangle formed by Ginsberg's *Howl*, the Book of Lamentations, and hip-hop. When Charles and the students finished applauding, they asked Hector to say the poem again, and he did. Later Charles told me, "That kid is the real thing." Hector's discomfort with Sylvia and me turned to ease. He came to our house for a small Christmas party and at other times. We talked on the telephone about a scholarship program and about what steps he should take next in his education. I came to know his parents. As a student, he began quietly, almost secretly, to surpass many of his classmates.

Timothy Koranda was the most professorial of the professors. He arrived precisely on time, wearing a hat of many styles—part fedora, part Borsalino, part Stetson, and at least one-half World War I campaign hat. He taught logic during class hours, filling the blackboard from floor to ceiling, wall to wall, drawing the intersections of sets here and truth tables there and a great square of oppositions in the middle of it all. After class, he walked with students to the subway, chatting about Zen or logic or Heisenberg.

On one of the coldest nights of the winter, he introduced the students to logic problems stated in ordinary language that they could solve by reducing the phrases to symbols. He passed out copies of a problem, two pages long, then wrote out some of the key phrases on the blackboard. "Take this home with you," he said, "and at our next meeting we shall see who has solved it. I shall also attempt to find the answer."

By the time he finished writing out the key phrases, however, David Iskhakov raised his hand. Although they listened attentively, neither David nor his sister Susana spoke often in class. She was shy, and he was embarrassed at his inability to speak perfect English.

"May I go to blackboard?" David said. " And will see if I have found correct answer to zis problem."

Together Tim and David erased the blackboard; then David began covering it with signs and symbols. "If first man is earning this money, and second man is closer to this town . . .," he said, carefully laying out the conditions. After five minutes or so, he said, "And the answer is: B will get first to Cleveland!"

Samantha Smoot shouted, "That's not the answer. The mistake you made is in the first part there, where it says who earns more money."

Tim folded his arms across his chest, happy. "I shall let you all take the problem home," he said.

When Sylvia and I left the Clemente Center that night, a knot of students was gathered outside, huddled against the wind. Snow had begun to fall, a slippery powder on the gray ice that covered all but a narrow space down the center of the sidewalk. Samantha and David stood in the middle of the group, still arguing over the answer to the problem. I leaned in for a moment to catch the character of the argument. It was even more polite than it had been in the classroom, because now they governed themselves.

One Saturday morning in January, David Howell telephoned me at home. "Mr. Shores," he said, anglicizing my name, as many of the students did.

"Mr. Howell," I responded, recognizing his voice.

"How you doin', Mr. Shores?"

"I'm fine. How are you?"

"I had a little problem at work."

Uh-oh, I thought; bad news was coming. David is a big man, generally good-humored but with a quick temper. According to his mother, he had a history of violent behavior. In the classroom he had been one of the best students, a steady man, twenty-four years old, who always did the reading assignments and who often made interesting connections between the humanities and daily life. "What happened?"

"Mr. Shores, there's a woman at my job, she said some things to me and I said some things to her. And she told my supervisor I had said things to her, and he called me in about it. She's forty years old and she don't have no social life, and she's jealous of me."

"And then what happened?" The tone of his voice and the timing of the call did not portend good news.

"Mr. Shores, she made me so mad, I wanted to smack her up against the wall. I tried to talk to some friends to calm myself down a little, but nobody was around."

"And what did you do?" I asked, fearing this was his one telephone call from the city jail.

"Mr. Shores, I asked myself, 'What would Socrates do?'"

David Howell had reasoned that his co-worker's envy was not his problem after all, and he had dropped his rage.

One evening, in the American History section, I was telling the students about Gordon Wood's ideas in *The Radicalism of the American Revolution*. We were talking about the revolt by some intellectuals against classical learning at the turn of the eighteenth century, including Benjamin Franklin's late-life change of heart, when Henry Jones raised his hand.

"If the Founders loved the humanities so much, how come they treated the natives so badly?"

I didn't know how to answer this question. There were confounding explanations to offer about changing attitudes toward Native Americans, vaguely useful references to views of Rousseau and James Fenimore Cooper. For a moment I wondered if I should tell them about Heidegger's Nazi past. Then I saw Abel Lomas's raised hand at the far end of the table, "Mr. Lomas," I said.

Abel said, "That's what Aristotle means by incontinence, when you know what's morally right but you don't do it, because you're overcome by your passions."

The other students nodded. They were all inheritors of wounds caused by the incontinence of educated men; now they had an ally in Aristotle, who had given them a way to analyze the actions of their antagonists.

Those who appreciate ancient history understand the radical character of the humanities. They know that politics did not begin in a perfect world but in a society even more flawed than ours: one that embraced slavery, denied the rights of women, practiced a form of homosexuality that verged on pedophilia, and endured the intrigues and corruption of its leaders. The genius of that society originated in man's re-creation of himself through the recognition of his humanness as expressed in art, literature, rhetoric, philosophy, and the unique notion of freedom. At that moment, the isolation of the private life ended and politics began.

The winners in the game of modern society, and even those whose fortune falls in the middle, have other means to power: they are included at birth. They know this. And they know exactly what to do to protect their place in the economic and social hierarchy. As Allan Bloom, author of the nationally best-selling tract in defense of elitism, *The Closing of the American Mind*, put it, they direct the study of the humanities exclusively at those young people who "have been raised in comfort and with the expectation of ever increasing comfort."

In the last meeting before graduation, the Clemente students answered the same set of questions they'd answered at orientation. Between October and May, students had fallen to AIDS, pregnancy, job opportunities, pernicious anemia, clinical depression, a schizophrenic child, and other forces, but of the thirty students admitted to the course, sixteen had completed it, and fourteen had earned credit from Bard College. Dr. Inclan found that the students' self-esteem and their abilities to divine and solve problems had significantly increased; their use of verbal aggression as a tactic for resolving conflicts had significantly decreased. And they all had notably more appreciation for the concepts of benevolence, spirituality, universalism, and collectivism.

It cost about $2,000 for a student to attend the Clemente Course. Compared with unemployment, welfare, or prison, the humanities are a bargain. But coming into possession of the faculty of reflection and the skills of politics leads to a choice for the poor—and whatever they choose, they will be dangerous: they may use politics to get along in a society based on the game, to escape from the surround of force into a gentler life, to behave as citizens, and nothing more; or they may choose to oppose the game itself. No one can predict the effect of politics, although we all would like to think that wisdom goes our way. That is why the poor are so often mobilized and so rarely politicized. The possibility that they will adopt a moral view other than that of their mentors can never be discounted. And who wants to run that risk?

On the night of the first Clemente Course graduation, the students and their families filled the eighty-five chairs we crammed into the conference room where classes had been held. Robert Martin, associate dean of Bard College, read the graduates' names. David Dinkins, the former mayor of New York City, handed out the diplomas. There were speeches and presentations. The students gave me a plaque on which they had misspelled my name. I offered a few words about each student, congratulated them, and said finally, "This is what I wish for you: May you never be more active than when you are doing nothing . . ." I saw their smiles of recognition at the words of Cato which I had written on the blackboard early in the course. They could recall again too the moment when we had come to the denouement of Aristotle's brilliantly constructed thriller, the *Nicomachean Ethics*—the idea that in the contemplative life man was most like God. One or two, perhaps more of the students, closed their eyes. In the momentary stillness of the room it was possible to think.

The Clemente Course in the Humanities ended a second year in June 1997. Twenty-eight new students had enrolled; fourteen graduated. Another version of the course will begin this fall in Yucatan, Mexico, using classical Maya literature in Maya.

On May 14, 1997, Viniece Walker came up for parole for the second time. She had served more than ten years of her sentence, and she had been the best of prisoners. In a version of the Clemente Course held at the prison she had been my teaching assistant. After a brief hearing, her request for parole was denied. She will serve two more years before the parole board will reconsider her case.

A year after graduation, ten of the first sixteen Clemente Course graduates were attending four-year colleges or going to nursing school; four of them had received full scholarships to Bard College. The other graduates were attending community college or working full-time. Except for one: she had been fired from her job in a fast-food restaurant for trying to start a union.

JOAN DIDION

WHY I WRITE

Of course I stole the title for this talk from George Orwell. One reason I stole it was that I like the sound of the words: *Why I Write*. There you have three short unambiguous words that share a sound, and the sound they share is this:

I

I

I

In many ways writing is the act of saying *I*, of imposing oneself upon other people of saying *listen to me, see it my way, change your mind*. It's an aggressive, even a hostile act. You can disguise its aggressiveness all you want with veils of subordinate clauses and qualifiers and tentative subjunctives, with ellipses and evasions—with the whole manner of intimating rather than claiming, of alluding rather than stating—but there's no getting around the fact that setting words on paper is the tactic of a secret bully, an invasion, an imposition of the writer's sensibility on the reader's most private space.

I stole the title not only because the words sounded right but because they seemed to sum up, in a no-nonsense way, all I have to tell you. Like many writers I have only this one "subject," this one "area": the act of writing. I can bring you no reports from any other front. I may have other interests: I am "interested," for example, in marine biology, but I don't flatter myself that you would come out to hear me talk about it. I am not a scholar. I am not in the least an intellectual, which is not to say that when I hear the word "intellectual" I reach for my gun, but only to say that I do not think in abstracts. During the years when I was an undergraduate at Berkeley I tried, with a kind of hopeless late-adolescent energy, to buy some temporary visa into the world of ideas, to forge for myself a mind that could deal with the abstract.

In short I tried to think. I failed. My attention veered inexorably back to the specific, to the tangible, to what was generally considered, by everyone I knew then and for that matter have known since, the peripheral. I would try to contemplate the Hegelian dialectic and would find myself concentrating instead on a flowering pear tree outside my window and the particular way the petals fell on my floor. I would try to read linguistic theory and would find myself wondering instead if the lights were on in the bevatron up the hill. When I say that I was wondering if the lights were on in the bevatron you might immediately suspect, if you deal in ideas at all, that I was registering the bevatron as a political symbol, thinking in shorthand about the military-industrial complex and its role in the university community, but you would be wrong. I was only wondering if the lights were on in the bevatron, and how they looked. A physical fact.

I had trouble graduating from Berkeley, not because of this inability to deal with ideas—I was majoring in English, and I could locate the house-and-garden imagery in *The Portrait of a Lady* as well as the next person, "imagery" being by definition the kind of specific that got my attention—but simply because I had neglected to take a course in Milton. For reasons which now sound baroque I needed a degree by the end of that summer, and the English department finally agreed, if I would come down from Sacramento every Friday and talk about the cosmology of *Paradise Lost*, to certify me proficient in Milton. I did this. Some Fridays I took the Greyhound bus, other Fridays I caught the Southern Pacific's City of San Francisco on the last leg of its transcontinental trip. I can no longer tell you whether Milton put the sun or the earth at the center of his universe in *Paradise Lost*, the central question of at least one century and a topic about which I wrote ten thousand words that summer, but I can still recall the exact rancidity of the butter in the City of San Francisco's dining car, and the way the tinted windows on the Greyhound bus cast the oil refineries around Carquinez Straits into a grayed and obscurely sinister light. In short my attention was always on the periphery, and what I would see and taste and touch, on the butter, and the Greyhound bus. During those years I was traveling on what I know to be a very shaky passport, forged papers: I knew that I was no legitimate resident in any world of ideas. I knew I couldn't think. All I knew then was what I couldn't do. All I knew then was what I wasn't, and it took me some years to discover what I was.

Which was a writer.

By which I mean not a "good" writer or a "bad" writer but simply a writer, a person whose most absorbed and passionate hours are spent arranging words on pieces of paper. Had my credentials been in order I would never have become a writer. Had I been blessed with even limited access to my own mind there would have been no reason to write. I write entirely to find out what I'm thinking, what I'm looking at, what I see and what it means. What I want and what I fear. Why did the oil refineries around Carquinez Straits seem sinister to me in the summer of 1956? Why have the night lights in the bevatron burned in my mind for twenty years? *What is going on in these pictures in my mind?*

When I talk about pictures in my mind I am talking, quite specifically, about images that shimmer around the edges. There used to be an illustration in every elementary psychology book showing a cat drawn by a patient in varying stages of schizophrenia. This cat had a shimmer around it. You could see the molecular structure breaking down at the very edges of the cat: the cat became the background and the background the cat, everything interacting, exchanging ions. People on hallucinogens describe the same perception of objects. I'm not a schizophrenic, nor do I take hallucinogens, but certain images do shimmer for me. Look hard enough, and you can't miss the shimmer. It's there. You can't think too much about these pictures that shimmer. You just lie low and let them develop. You stay quiet. You don't talk to many people and you keep your nervous system from shorting out and you try to locate the cat in the shimmer, the grammar in the picture.

Just as I meant "shimmer" literally I mean "grammar" literally. Grammar is a piano I play by ear, since I seem to have been out of school the year the rules were mentioned. All I know about grammar is its infinite power. To shift the structure of a sentence alters the meaning of that sentence, as definitely and inflexibly as the position of a camera alters the meaning of the object photographed. Many people know about camera angles now, but not so many know about sentences. The arrangement of the words matters, and the arrangement you want can be found in the picture in your mind. The picture dictates the arrangement. The picture dictates whether this will be a sentence with or without clauses, a sentence that ends hard or a dying-fall sentence, long or short, active or passive. The picture tells you how to arrange the words and the arrangement of the words tells you, or tells me what's going on in the picture. *Nota bene*:

It tells you. You don't tell it.

Let me show you what I mean by pictures in the mind. I began *Play It as It Lays* just as I have begun each of my novels, with no notion of "character" or "plot" or even "incident." I had only two pictures in my mind, more about which later, and a technical intention, which was to write a novel so elliptical and fast that it would be over before you noticed it, a novel so fast that it would scarcely exist on the page at all. About the pictures: the first was of white space. Empty space. This was clearly the picture that dictated the narrative intention of the book—a book in which anything that happened would happen off the page, a "white" book to which the reader would have to bring his or her own bad dreams—and yet this picture told me no "story," suggested no situation. The second picture did. This second picture was of something actually witnessed. A young woman with long hair and a short white halter dress walks through the casino at the Riviera in Las Vegas at one in the morning. She crosses the casino alone and picks up a house telephone. I watch her because I have heard her paged, and recognize her name: she is a minor actress I see around Los Angeles from time to time, in places like Jax and once in a gynecologist's office in the Beverly Hills Clinic, but have never met. I know nothing about her. Who is paging her? Why is she here to be paged? How exactly did she come to this? It was precisely this moment in Las Vegas that made *Play It as It Lays* begin to tell itself to me, but the moment appears in the novel only obliquely, in a chapter which begins:

Maria made a list of things she would never do. She would never: walk through the Sands or Caesar's alone after midnight. She would never: ball at a party, do S-M unless she wanted to, borrow furs from Abe Lipsey, deal. She would never: carry a Yorkshire in Beverly Hills.

That is the beginning of the chapter and that is also the end of the chapter, which may suggest what I meant by "white space."

I recall having a number of pictures in my mind when I began the novel I just finished, *A Book of Common Prayer*. As a matter of fact one of these pictures was of that bevatron I mentioned, although I would be hard put to tell you a story in which nuclear energy figured. Another was a newspaper photograph of a hijacked 707 burning on the desert in the Middle East. Another was the night view from a room in which I once spent a week with paratyphoid, a hotel room on the Colombian coast. My husband and I seemed to be on the Colombian coast representing the United States of America at a film festival (I recall invoking the name "Jack Valenti" a lot, as if its reiteration could make me well), and it was a bad place to have fever, not only because my indisposition offended our hosts but because every night in this hotel the generator failed. The lights went out. The elevator stopped. My husband would go to the event of the evening and make excuses for me and I would stay alone in this hotel room, in the dark. I remember standing at the window trying to call Bogota (the telephone seemed to work on the same principle as the generator) and watching the night wind come up and wonder what I was doing eleven degrees off the equator with a fever of 103. The view from that window definitely figures in *A Book of Common Prayer*, as does the burning 707, and yet none of these pictures told me the story I needed.

The picture that did, the picture that shimmered and made these other images coalesce, was the Panama airport at 6 a.m. I was in this airport only once, on a plane to Bogota that stopped for an hour to refuel, but the way it looked that morning remained superimposed on everything I saw until the day I finished *A Book of Common Prayer*. I lived in that airport for several years. I can still feel the hot air when I step off the plane, can see the heat already rising off the tarmac at 6 a.m. I can feel my skirt damp and wrinkled on my legs. I can feel the asphalt stick to my sandals. I remember the big tail of a Pan American plane floating motionless down at the end of the tarmac. I remember the sound of a slot machine in the waiting room. I could tell you that I remember a particular woman in the airport, an American woman, a *norteamericana*, a thin *norteamericana* about forty who wore a big square emerald in lieu of a wedding ring, but there was no such woman there.

I put this woman in the airport later. I made this woman up, just as I later make up a country to put the airport in, and a family to run the country. This woman in the airport is neither catching a plane nor meeting one. She is ordering tea in the airport coffee shop. In fact she is not simply "ordering" tea but insisting that the water be boiled, in front of her, for twenty minutes. Why is this woman in this airport? Why is she going nowhere; where has she been? Where did she get that big emerald? What derangement, or disassociation, makes her believe that her will to see the water boiled can possibly prevail?

> She had been going to one airport or another for four months, one could see it, looking at the visas on her passport. All those airports where Charlotte Douglas's passport had been stamped would have looked alike. Sometimes the sign on the tower would say "Bienvenidos" and sometimes the sign on the tower would say "Bienvenue," some places were wet and hot and others dry and hot, but at each of these airports the pastel concrete walls would rust and stain and the swamp off the runway would be littered with the fuselages of cannibalized Fairchild F-227's and the water would need boiling.
>
> "I knew why Charlotte went to the airport even if Victor did not."
>
> "I knew about airports."

These lines appear about halfway through *A Book of Common Prayer*, but I wrote them during the second week I worked on the book, long before I had any idea where Charlotte Douglas had been or why she went to airports. Until I wrote these lines I had no character called "Victor" in mind: the necessity for mentioning a name, and the name "Victor," occurred to me as I wrote the sentence. *I knew why Charlotte went to the airport* sounded incomplete. *I knew why Charlotte went to the airport even if Victor did not* carried a little more narrative drive. Most important of all, until I wrote these lines I did not know who "I" was, who was telling the story. I had intended until that moment that the "I" be no more than the voice of the author, a 19th-century omniscient narrator. But there it was:

> "I knew why Charlotte went to the airport even if Victor did not."
> "I knew about airports."

This "I" was the voice of no author in my house. This "I" was someone who not only knew why Charlotte went to the airport but also knew someone called "Victor." Who was Victor? Who was this narrator? Why was this narrator telling me this story? Let me tell you one thing about why writers write: had I known the answer to any of these questions I would never have needed to write a novel.

PETER SACKS

THE POSTMODERN SPECTACLE AND GENERATION X

When Mick was a third-grader, he gave an oral report to his classmates about his travels to Europe as a youngster. For a few minutes, Mick says, he was the center of attention, the stories of his travels enrapturing his classmates. But afterward, nobody mentioned his trip again. Mick went on in later years to travel around the world, and when the subject of his traveling adventures would come up in casual conversation with his peers in junior high and high school, he says the common response was simply: "Oh." Then, like clockwork, the conversation would inevitably go on to the next subject. "This has been a huge influence on my life," Mick, a nineteen-year-old college student, told me. "The fact that I was a world traveler, that was just a bit of information about Mick." I asked him why his peers refused to dwell on anything for very long, such as his travels, obviously an important part of who he was. "Maybe it's because they never really had to think about something," he says. "It's like playing a video game; you just turn it off. You don't have to dwell on your defeat, you just start over again."

As Mick told me this, I suddenly felt a surge of empathy toward him. I never knew that I could feel such kinship for a guy who was born the year I graduated from high school. "Oh." The moment he uttered that sound of indifference, I felt the rush of horrible memories from my first days of teaching, when I hadn't yet developed that crusty layer that I imagine many teachers must have to grow in order to keep from having a nervous breakdown during class. Though I too have grown the crust, I've never really gotten over the feelings of inadequacy those brutal, passive stares can still give me.

That look of indifference that threw me into culture shock when I became a teacher might be the mirror image of the magnificent spectacle of images that have nurtured GenXers from childhood. Colorful, mesmerizing images and sounds flash and go; at a child's whim Big Bird metamorphoses into Mr. Brady, who in turn is transformed into an MTV sex object. The spectacle that Generation X was born watching is never boring—the hand-held remote guarantees that much.

In *Brave New World*, Aldous Huxley foresaw a society whose inhabitants had repudiated thinking and reflection for the constant desire to be amused. It seems that Huxley's world has arrived with a vengeance in the postmodern epoch of spectacular America. Generation X, like Huxley's babes who were nurtured with "hypnopaedia," have grown to expect amusement in virtually every aspect of their lives. Although the human desire to be entertained, to be provoked and engaged is good and natural, many of my students sometimes expected entertainment to the exclusion of almost everything else. Their desire to be entertained seemed at times a low but constant background buzz, providing the real cultural context that shaped virtually everything that went on in the classroom. It was as if I felt the constant force of Madonna's breasts or Michael Jackson's deft hand in his crotch, which I somehow had to live up to in order to hold my students' attention, in order to keep the brutal and indifferent "Oh" at bay.

To be sure, not all college professors would agree with the assertion that students just want to be entertained. Many might contend that they don't see direct evidence of students' desires for amusement in their classrooms. Besides the sea of indifferent stares I faced each day, I can point to my own modest survey in which four in ten students picked "entertaining" as the most important quality for their teachers (see chapter 6). I can cite a study of 135 students at one Midwestern university in which students equated learning and good teaching with "entertainment." I can point to the many complaints I heard from my colleagues, like this one: "The TV generation expects to entertained. With an attention span equal to the interval between commercials, that is not surprising." But I can also point to the words of students themselves, who in one way or another told me that the amusement culture has been a central force in defining their generation.

Lloyd, the twenty-eight-year-old recent graduate I mentioned earlier, who now works in computer sales, told me, "If there's a unifying force of our generation, it's TV." He gestured around the coffeehouse we were in, which was full of twentysomethings and students from the nearby college. "I could get a heated debate going right now if I blurted out, 'So who is more macho, Kirk or Picard?'" Lloyd said. "I find that kind of strange."

Marsha, a young woman who seemed mature beyond her twenty years, who was studying at a local community college, said, "We're a society that has grown up watching TV, going for the fast laugh, the quick entertainment. It's rare to find somebody who just sits and reads and goes bird watching. You're more likely to find somebody in front of TV nowadays. That has an effect on the classroom. Students expect to be entertained. If it's not entertaining, or something you feel passionate about, it's easy to tune out."

Angie, an eighteen-year-old freshman who wants to study marine biology, told me what she wanted from her teachers: "Last year, I took a speech class, which was completely boring. There are so many other ways it could be more interesting. Anything other than just lecture. Something more humorous, you know? Lectures are just one person talking, and it's kind of just not really any tone. Something that's loud and nashes or something like that, it grabs your attention. When somebody is just standing there just talking, it makes you want to fall asleep." Then, in the next breath, Angie said, "I think the media is out of control. Technology is moving so fast. We need to take a breath and stop for while and give people time to catch up."

When I asked Frederick, a former student of mine, what he wanted in his teachers, he was blunt: "We want you guys to dance, sing, and cry. Seriously, that is what we consider to be good learning. We expect so much more from everything now because of the media. You guys can't compete."

As I've already discussed, postmodernity has delegitimated the authorities of the modern era, not the least of which have been educators. There might well be numerous specific reasons educational institutions have been debased. But it seems plausible that some of the depreciation in the worth of teachers has been a consequence of our culture's abiding faith in entertainment. Like Denzel Washington's character well understood in *Crimson Tide*, reproduced images of reality had become more real, more meaningful, and far less scary than reality itself for Generation X. "Higher education doesn't work any more," Frederick told me. "lt doesn't challenge. We (students) think the media is more substantial than you the teacher. We don't value what teachers say and do. We're afraid of what you will say and do; it's so personal. With media it's so impersonal. We don't want to be personal any more with anybody. We don't want to confront our emotions. Machines are easier. If we can get it from machines, we don't have to get it from a person. The media is passive, safer. It doesn't really affect us. But a teacher, it's real, it's close."

Marketing and media types have understood well Frederick's suggestion that mediated reality can be far more persuasive than reality itself for a generation that learned to read on *Sesame Street*. Protestations about the "myth" of Generation X notwithstanding, corporate America knows that Xers are perhaps the most media savvy, image-conscious cohort, ever. Never has a single age group been so well attended to and fussed over in the media, with entire television networks and much of the magazine industry devoted to the X group. There's the obvious, such as MTV, but also the upstart Fox network whose programming is dominated by shows predominately for Xers (that is, *Beverly Hills 90210*, *Melrose Place*, *The X-Files*, *Party of Five*— the list goes on and is getting bigger). There is cable's FX channel, sort of an MTV with half a brain and a toned-down sex drive, and a slough of magazines dedicated to Xers, drooling over the $95 billion they'll spend annually on everything from Teen Spirit to Mountain Dew.

But don't count out the establishment media as well. From My *So-Called Life* and NBC's *Friends* to the local daily serving up special "Teen" pages in their Saturday papers, presented in the Gen X code of what's cool, the old guard, too, is doing back flips to attract Xers. One of my favorite examples is *marie claire* magazine, which ran a series of full-pagers in the *New York Times* (aimed at advertisers, no doubt). In one ad, a cooly attired, very attractive X girl, shirt unbuttoned to her waist, is slumped in a chair, and she's complaining about all the useless white noise out there coming from other fashion and glamour magazines that she's now decided to shut out. But *marie claire*, on the other hand, "talks the talk." The X girl, she's very cool, and so by implication is *marie claire* a joint venture backed by none other than the Hearst Corporation.

Indeed, so overpowering has become the force of amusement in our culture that institutions of modernity are, chameleon-like, clothing themselves in a postmodern guise, trying to "talk the talk." Take, for example, American religious institutions. Many are transforming themselves into corporate-like enterprises that are pushing sort of a "Bible-Lite" to attract Baby Boomers and Generation Xers. Some churches, not unlike a high-powered advertising agency might, are hiring marketing specialists savvy about the twentysomething mentality, to recruit new churchgoers bored with traditional church stuff. "How in the world could we ever create something so exciting in church, where people would wait four and a half hours to get in?" says the Rev. Walt Kallestad of Phoenix, referring to a line of people he once saw for a Batman movie. That experience inspired his new approach to religion as amusement. "Entertainment is really the medium of the day," he says.

For obvious reasons, elementary, junior high, and high schools have been far quicker to adapt the amusement culture to the educational setting than has higher education. Elementary education is, after all, the sort of environment where the phenomenon of teachers running around in chicken costumes is held up to be an example of "innovative" teaching. "Whether it is rented from a video store, purchased from a catalog, or taped off the air waves, visual media has become as common as textbooks and chalk in history/social science classrooms," says one California high school teacher. But primary education, having pandered to children's desires for amusement, has created a generation of twentysomethings who now expect the same treatment at colleges and universities.

Judging by educational journals, the demands by students to be entertained has produced a sharp split among educators in colleges and universities about how far teachers should go to pander to the new generation. The following is an example taken from a book for new college teachers, in which one professor offers advice on the "entertainment issue." As perhaps the dominant viewpoint in educational circles, the writer seems to suggest that it's the teacher's responsibility to deal with whatever students dish out in terms of low interest and motivation. Students' desires for entertainment has become a fact of life and teachers must cope with it—and better to be amusing than boring. The author writes:

> Most of the time what motivates faculty to discuss the entertainment issue is not the role it does or does not play in student learning but their own discomfort with this 'performance' dimension of teaching. Many of us find it hard to envision ourselves doing a Jonny Carson or Joan Rivers routine, coming to class in costumes, or dancing before students as some of our more dramatic colleagues have been known to do. But the question here is really one of degree. There are lots of steps on the way to becoming a Carson or Rivers. Most of us have hardly taken more than a step or two in that direction. We don't err on the side of too much entertaining. We err more often on the side of boring.

Reasoning such as this makes me afraid that college and university classrooms are in danger of becoming mere extensions of the rest of spectacular, pop-America. And it appears that some people in higher education are ready to go even further down the slippery slope of amusement, beginning to adopt the same rhetoric as their counterparts in elementary education, that good teaching is tantamount to entertainment. Indeed, to be entertaining is a sign of "professionalism," in the view of some. Take for example Richard Wolkomir's assessment of "Old Jearl," as students called physics instructor Jearl Walker, who "has been known to lecture in costumes, stick balloons on his forehead, and even plunge his bare hand into a pot of molten lead," according to some observers. Says Wolkomir: "Walker's antics may strike some pedagogues as a clear case of pandering to the modern student's desire for instant entertainment. But at a time when the nation is once again reassessing its educational means and ends, his commitment and creativity may suggest to others a new standard of professionalism and new possibilities for enlivening curricula in the humanities as well as the sciences." In what appears to be an increasingly common sentiment within higher education, the authors of one educational journal article concluded: "If effective teachers are entertaining teachers, and today's media-saturated students expect to be entertained and cannot tolerate boredom, then it is time to underscore the need for entertainment in the classroom."

Of course, most of the students I talked to tell me they would welcome a proliferation of the spectacular in the classroom. They say, for instance, that watching something on a video is easier and more engaging than reading a book or listening to a lecture. From my experience, many students have come to equate the mere fact that they're "engaged" with the illusion of real learning. But that students might be engaged—i.e., not bored—doesn't necessarily mean that they're doing any real thinking. The sad fact is that most students don't know how to think because, as Mick told me, they've never had to in almost any aspect of their lives. When you've grown up locked on to the spectacle, notions of truth, reality, and substance recede into meaninglessness. What is meaningful is what is momentarily before your eyes. Says the French writer Guy Debord, in his *Comments on the Society of the Spectacle*: "When social significance is attributed only to what is immediate, and to what will be immediate immediately afterwards, always replacing another, identical immediacy, it can be seen that the uses of the media guarantee a kind of eternity of noisy insignificance."

For the culture at large, but especially for Generation X, one more image or fact is all just "one more bit of information," as Mick would say: Whether it's about O.J. Simpson, the campaign for President, or the Bosnian War, each one engenders yet another collective "Oh." Says Mick: "I have an older friend who says when he was young, he'd watch a news clip at the movies, and he'd have a couple of weeks to think about it. Today we get that short bit of information over breakfast, three times a day, just driving down the street. There's so much information, we can't distinguish what to think about and what's just b.s. There's just too much of it, and we don't have time to think."

COOL IS AS COOL DOES

Of course, it's one thing not having time or inclination to think because there's too much to think about. It's quite another matter refusing to think, indeed, revelling in one's choosing not to think.

Once I had a student who did a movie review of the film, *Nobody's Fool*, about a cantankerous character living in a small town in upstate New York played by Paul Newman. The student panned the movie. Why? She said the plot wasn't entertaining. In fact, her *only* criterion for evaluating this film was that it wasn't entertaining enough, that there wasn't enough action. That there might be other ways to view a film, such as character development, mood, realism, etc., never occurred to her nor most others in the class. When I pointed out to students that there might be other ways to look at a film besides its entertainment value, blank looks of indifference swept though the room. It was as if they were reacting viscerally to the notion of complexity—that their set view of the world was being challenged. "Who cares?" seemed to be the collective response. But what was most disturbing for me was that they seemed *proud* of their ignorance.

Another time, I tried to underscore for students why it was important to read the newspaper every day. It was becoming obvious to me that, even though they had purchased the newspaper for my class, few were actually reading it, despite the fact that I quizzed on current affairs. On a five-question quiz, the clear majority would often get all five wrong. I wanted to shock them, to embarrass them actually, with their own ignorance of public life. So, I tried another little quiz, this one not based on any particular events. I asked students to tell me what G.O.P. meant and who it referred to. I also asked them how much welfare spending contributed to the federal budget. On the former I got such answers as "Great Old Politics," "Part of a Government," "Gross Product," and this winner: "Goopy Old People." And according to my students, the U.S. government is spending a whopping 30 to 50 percent of the federal budget on welfare. (It's actually just 1 percent.) But my students were hardly embarrassed. It seemed that the few students who got the answers nearly right were considered by their peers to be nerds and freaks. It was cool to be, if not dumb, to act as if ignorance of public affairs was a sign that you were too cool for all that serious grown-up garbage.

In the cafeteria-style approach to values that characterizes postmodernity, add a healthy serving of anti-intellectualism to the cynicism, paranoia, and anti-rationality that millions of Americans are adopting as their guiding principles nowadays. While the larger culture embraces anti-intellectualism as simply a sort of healthy, All American trait, Generation X is putting its own spin on the old idea that ignorance is bliss: It's also very cool.

To the extent that the postmodern generation traffics above all else in entertainment values, popular culture, and image, they are being inundated with the screwy idea that there's little to be gained from being smart. Why, you might end up being like Bill Clinton, the Yale Law School and Oxford grad whom media pundits flippantly refer to as "the smartest guy in the class." Educators, intellectuals, and opinion leaders commonly say that we live in an age of no heroes, which is perfect nonsense when you consider how extravagantly and unflinchingly our culture worships the likes of Michael Jordan, Bruce Willis, and Tom Hanks. I'm not saying actors and athletes aren't smart, but we surely don't idolize them for their beautiful brains. It's worth noting again that the smart guy who conceived and wrote the book and screenplay *Forrest Gump* earned for his work on the film about 1 percent of Hanks's $31 million as an actor in the movie. And let's not forget the Gump phenomenon itself. Among the most popular movies of all time, *Forrest Gump* idealizes naive stupidity as something to strive for in life. It pays handsomely.

Indeed, as opposed to the goodness of Gump, smart guys are often the bad guys in the movies. Really smart guys are either innocent buffoons, such as Walter Matthau's Einstein in *IQ*, mad bombers like Jeremy Iron's character in *Die Hard with a Vengeance* or shrewd profiteers like Michael Douglas's character in *Wall Street*, you're not really up to hero quality in our culture unless you're someone of medium intelligence who is "able to get the better of the twisted genius," observes Phillip Lopate, a professor of literature at Hofstra University.

Of course, what I'm about to suggest might mean nothing of much significance. But then again, it might say something about the state of our culture when, as reported in the *New York Times*, celebrities, such as Neil Diamond, Michael Bolton, and Barbara Streisand, topped the charts as the most frequent speakers at college commencement ceremonies in the spring of 1995. Who says Generation X has no heroes?

The anti-intellectual juggernaut that Generation X watches at the movies and on TV is one thing, but also consider what they get increasingly from my own field of journalism, which—to the surprise of many of my students—traditionally has stood alongside higher education as one of the pillars of modernity. At its best, the American press has stood for emancipatory values, justice, and truth-seeking. But much of mainstream journalism is becoming just another aspect of the spectacle, pandering to audiences that demand amusement. In what former *Washington Post* writer Carl Bernstein has called the "triumph of the Idiot Culture," the ideals of truth, justice, and emancipation have become almost meaningless, mere verbiage that professional journalism organizations quaintly place in their codes of ethics. "For the first time in our history, the weird and the stupid and the coarse are becoming our cultural norm, even our ideal," says Bernstein, the guy who helped uncover the Watergate scandal. Of course, one reason newspapers have turned to gross simplicity and the sensational is to attract younger people who don't read, and so print journalism has tried to be more like TV, becoming more simple to attract readers who *still* won't read the paper. Most newspapers' brilliant response to this trend is to try to become even more entertaining, and so on in a vicious circle.

Indeed, the postmodern generation could be the most disengaged cohort in the history of the republic. According to a recent study by the Higher Education Research Institute at UCLA, today's college freshmen are the least interested in public affairs of any group of freshmen in the institute's twenty-nine-year history of measuring this trait. Just one in three college freshmen indicated that keeping up with public affairs was important to them, compared to six in ten freshmen who thought so in 1966.

Robert Pollack, a professor of biology and former dean at Columbia University, says young people are rationalizing their ignorance because the world is too complex to cope with. Pollack might be a bit more charitable than I when he says he's noticed many students maintain a "willful naivete . . . in the face of a complicated world," a "wish to remain innocent: If I don't understand the complexity, it doesn't bother me," says Pollack. Students nowadays, he says, would rather see the world as "a place to outwit, not a place to help run."

Meantime, Xers are inventing their own postmodern journalistic forms in an effort to talk their own talk, quite apart from the co-opting influence of corporate media. GenXers have typecast newspapers and traditional print media as boring, and mainstream papers won't attract the postmodern generation unless they transform themselves into something entirely new. Recognizing this obviousness, Xers themselves are giving us new magazines and newspapers like Dallas's *The Met*. Who is *The Met* trying to reach? "My reader doesn't care that city hall is stealing from us," twenty-four-year-old publisher Randy Stagen told the *Columbia Journalism Review*. "He cares that there's a great band playing tonight and that there's cold beer at Phil's Bar."

Or consider *Project X* magazine, subtitled "your global guide to tomorrow's scene." That subtitle says volumes about Generation X culture. We're not talking about *today's* scene here; just getting "now" right used to be what one wishing for cool could ever hope for. But in today's accelerated culture, we're seeing the spectacle unfold of an absurd competition for coolness in a world in which everybody has already seen and heard everything, and coolness has come to be defined as newer than new and beyond the now. Cool is *post*-postmodern, post-cyberspace, post-Internet. Cool is anti-present.

And the past? Well, it never existed, except perhaps in vintage clothing stores. Commenting on the latest, coolest, X-oriented magazines it had anointed, *Project X* wrote, "The hottest magazines of this season are here; they're post Generation X, post teen, post anything that marketing analysts can even begin to identify."

But try as the new Gen X media might to "cool" their way out of dominant culture's shadow, there's no escaping it. *Project X*, for example, using the fashionably convoluted, sometimes unreadable formats for its printed pages, despises the printed culture of modernism for a postmodern, anti-print design. But it's still print. It despises the commercialism of the dominant culture, but it still runs ads for Dewar's. But (slap me, I generalize), I would guess that the intended audience for this magazine and others like it are quite oblivious to such contradictions and, I dare say, manipulation. Growing up in a spectacular society that constantly reinforces the "ideals" of anti-intellectualism and vacuity, one learns not to see anything beyond its pretty face value. That's what the spectacle is all about—pure pleasure and pure entertainment. Which is why *Project X*s gambit that it can out-manipulate the masters of manipulation on Madison Avenue, won't work: In a spectacular culture, consumers don't care much that *marie claire* is really published by a bunch of boomers at the Hearst Corporation. Born into the postmodern spectacle, GenXers know no other language than the language of the spectacle; they know no other talk nor walk other than that of the spectacle; and by definition, the spectacle knows completely the language of the youth culture, who despite their efforts, will remain naive prisoners of conformity to the amusement society. Guy Debord says:

> The individual who has been more deeply marked by this impoverished spectacular thought than by any other aspect of his experience puts himself at the service of the established order right from the start, even though subjectively he may have had quite the opposite intention. He will essentially follow the language of the spectacle, for it is the only one he is familiar with; the one in which he learned to speak. No doubt he would like to be regarded as an enemy of its rhetoric; but he will use its syntax. This is one of the most important aspects of spectacular domination's success.

We've come a long way, then, since the days of Voltaire and Rousseau, when *enlightenment*, of all things, was cool. But then, ignorance and naivete might be a natural response to the wild spectacle of information and images careening out of control in postmodern America. Although I personally recoil at the "willful naivete," in Robert Pollack's words, that I observed in so many students, aren't these children of postmodernity simply a predictable creation of a larger culture that itself is recoiling from thinking and reflection? I'm unfortunately reminded of Aldous Huxley's words in *Brave New World* when he's describing the long-lasting results of the new society's conditioning of its offspring: "They'll grow up with what the psychologists used to call an instinctive, hatred of books and flowers. Reflexes unalterably conditioned. They'll be safe from books and botany all their lives."

ABIGAIL WITHERSPOON

THIS PEN FOR HIRE
On Grinding Out Papers
for College Students

I am an academic call girl. I write college kids' papers for a living. Term papers, book reports, senior theses, take-home exams. My "specialties": art history and sociology, international relations and comparative literature, English, psychology, "communications," Western philosophy (ancient and contemporary), structural anthropology; film history, evolutionary biology, waste management and disposal, media studies, and pre-Confederation Canadian history. I throw around allusions to Caspar Weinberger and Alger Hiss, Sacco and Vanzetti, Haldeman and Ehrlichman, Joel Steinberg and Baby M. The teaching assistants eat it up. I can do simple English or advanced jargon. Like other types of prostitutes, I am, professionally, very accommodating.

I used to tell myself I'd do this work only for a month or two, until I found something else. But the official unemployment rate in this large Canadian city where I live is almost 10 percent, and even if it were easy to find a job, I'm American, and therefore legally prohibited from receiving a paycheck. So each day I walk up the stairs of a rotting old industrial building to an office with a sign on the window: TAILORMADE ESSAYS, WRITING AND RESEARCH. The owner, whom I'll call Matthew, claims that he started the business for ghostwriters, speechwriters, and closet biographers, and only gradually moved into academic work as a sideline. But even Grace, the oldest surviving writer on Tailormade's staff, can't remember anybody ever writing much other than homework for students at one university or another.

This is a good city for Tailormade. Next door is the city's university and its tens of thousands of students, a school that was once somewhat better when not all of its computer-registered classes numbered in the hundreds. Orders come in from Vancouver, Calgary, Winnipeg. There are plenty of essay services in the States, of course; they advertise in campus newspapers and the back pages of music magazines. Some of the big ones have toll-free phone numbers. They're sprinkled all over: California, Florida, New Jersey. But we still get American business too. Orders come in here from Michigan, Vermont, Pennsylvania; from Illinois, Wisconsin, upstate New York, sometimes California; from Harvard, Cornell, and Brown. They come in from teachers' colleges, from people calling themselves "gifted students" (usually teenagers at boarding schools), and, once in a while, from the snazzy places some of our customers apparently vacation with their divorced dads, like Paris.

Matthew runs the business with his wife, Sylvia. Or maybe she is his ex-wife, nobody's exactly sure. When you call Tailormade—it's now in the phone book—you hear Sylvia say that Tailormade is Canada's foremost essay service; that our very qualified writers handle most academic subjects; and that we are fast, efficient, and completely confidential. Sylvia speaks loudly and slowly and clearly, especially to Asian customers. She is convinced that everyone who phones the office will be Asian, just as she's convinced that all Asians drive white Mercedes or black BMWs with cellular phones in them. From my personal experience, I find the Asian customers at least more likely to have done the assigned reading.

Matthew and Sylvia are oddly complementary. Matthew, gentle and fumbly, calls out mechanically, "Thank you, sir, ma'am, come again" after each departing back slinking down the hall. Sylvia asks the Chinese customers loudly, "SIMPLE ENGLISH?" She tells the uncertain, "Well, don't show up here till you know what you want," and demands of the dissatisfied, "Whaddya mean you didn't like it? You ordered it, din'cha?"

This afternoon, October 10, I'm here to hand in a paper and fight it out with the other writers for more assignments. Some of us are legal, some aren't.

Some have mortgages and cars, some don't. All of us are hungry. The office is jammed, since it's almost time for midterms. Tailormade does a brisk business from October to May, except for January. The chairs are full of customers studiously filling out order forms. You can always tell who is a student and who is a writer. The students are dressed elegantly and with precision; the writers wear ripped concert T-shirts or stained denim jackets with white undershirts peeking out. The students wear mousse and hair gel and nail polish and Tony Lama western boots and Tourneau watches and just the right amount of make-up. They smell of Escape, Polo for men, and gum. The writers smell of sweat, house pets, and crushed cigarettes. Four of the other writers are lolling in their chairs and fidgeting; work usually isn't assigned until all the order forms have been filled out, unless somebody requests a topic difficult to fill. Then Matthew will call out like an auctioneer: "Root Causes of the Ukrainian Famine? Second year? Anyone? Grace?" or "J. S. Mill's Brand of Humane Utilitarianism? Third year? Henry, that for you?" as some customer hovers in front of the desk, eyes straight ahead. Someone else in the room might idly remark that he or she took that course back in freshman year and it was a "gut" or a "real bird."

I suspect that each of us in the Tailormade stable of hacks sorts out the customers differently: into liberal arts students and business students; into those that at least do the reading and those that don't bother; into those that have trouble writing academic English and those that just don't care about school; into those that do their assignments in other subjects and those that farm every last one of them out to us; into the struggling and inept versus the rich, lazy, and stupid. But for Matthew and Sylvia, the clientele are divisible, even before cash versus credit card, or paid-up versus owing, into Asian customers and non-Asian ones. There's been an influx of wealthy immigrants from Hong Kong in recent years, fleeing annexation. Matthew and Sylvia seem to resent their presence and, particularly, their money. Yet they know that it's precisely this pool of customers—who have limited written English language skills but possess education, sophistication, ambition, cash, and parents leaning hard on them for good grades— that keeps the business going.

When I hand in my twelve pages on "The Role of Market Factors in the Development of the Eighteenth-Century Fur Trade," Matthew tells me,

"This lady's been patiently waiting without complaining." I must be very late. Turning to the client, he picks up one of my sheets and waves it. "At least it's a nice bib," he points out to her. "Look at that." Although I wasn't provided with any books for this essay, I managed to supply an extensive bibliography. I can't remember what I put on it.

I'm still waiting for an assignment. In fact, all the writers are still waiting. We often wait at the bar around the corner; Tailormade has its own table there, permanently reserved. But we all have to get ourselves to the office eventually to pick up assignments. Grace, the oldest writer and by now, probably, the best, sits sorrowfully by the window, her long gray hair falling into her lap and her head jammed into her turtleneck, on her thin face a look of permanent tragedy. Grace gets up at three in the morning to work; she never forgets a name, a fact, or an assignment; she has a deep, strange love for Japanese history and in ten years here has probably hatched enough pages and research for several doctoral dissertations in that field. Elliott, another writer, reclines near the door, his little dog asleep under his chair. He uses the dog as an icebreaker with the clients, especially young women. He is six and a half feet tall and from somewhere far up in the lunar landscape of northern Ontario. He has a huge head of blond hair down to his eyes and pants as tight as a rock star's. Elliott is the business writer. He specializes in finance, investment, management, and economics. He lives out of a suitcase; he and the little dog, perhaps practicing fiscal restraint, seem to stay with one of a series of girlfriends. When the relationship comes to an end, Elliott and the little dog wind up back in the office, where they sleep in the fax room and Elliott cranks out essays on his laptop. Henry and Russell, two other writers, twist around, changing position, the way travelers do when they're trying to nap on airport lounge chairs. They both look a little like El Greco saints, although perhaps it just seems that way to me because lately I've been doing a lot of art history papers. They both have long skinny legs, long thin white nervous twiddling hands, long thin faces with two weeks' worth of unintentional beard. Henry points out how good Russell looks, and we all agree. Russell is forty. He has a new girlfriend half his age who has, he says, provided a spiritual reawakening. Before he met her, Russell drank so much and held it so badly that he had the distinction of being the only staff member to be banned from the bar around the corner for life. Henry, by contrast, looks terrible. He's always sick, emaciated, coughing, but he invariably manages to meet his deadlines, to make his page quotas, and to show up on time. We used to have another writer on staff, older even than Russell or Grace, who smoked a pipe, nodded a lot, and never said anything. He was a professor who'd been fired from some school, we were never really sure where. Eventually, he went AWOL and started an essay-writing service of his own. He's now Tailormade's main competition. The only other competitors, apparently, worked out of a hot-dog stand parked next to a campus bookstore. Nobody knows whether they're open anymore.

In general, there is a furtiveness about the way we writers talk to one another, the way we socialize. In the office, we're a little like people who know each other from A.A. meetings or rough trade bars encountering each other on a Monday morning at the photocopy machine. It's not because we're competing for work. It's not even because some of us are illegal and everyone else knows it. It is, if anything, collective embarrassment. We know a lot more than Matthew and Sylvia do. They sit dumbly as we bullshit with the clients about their subjects and assignments ("Ah, introductory psychology! The evolution of psychotherapy is a fascinating topic . . . ever read a guy called Russell Jacoby?") in order to impress them and get them to ask for us. This must be the equivalent of the harlots' competitive bordello promenade. But we work for Matthew and Sylvia. They have the sense to pit us against each other, and it works. We can correct their pronunciation of "Goethe" and they don't care. They know it makes no difference. I suspect they have never been farther away than Niagara Falls; neither of them may have even finished high school. It doesn't matter. The laugh's on us, of course: they own the business.

OCTOBER 12, 1994. A tall gangly kid comes in for a twenty-page senior history essay about the ancient local jail. It involves research among primary sources in the provincial archives, and I spend a week there, going page by page through the faded brown script of the warden's prison logbooks of the 1830s. Agitators are being executed for "high treason" or "banished from the realm," which, I assume, means being deported. Once in a while there's a seductive joy to a project. You forget that you've undertaken it for money, that it isn't yours.

Most of the time, though, all I think about is the number of pages done, the number to go. Tailormade charges twenty dollars Canadian a page for first- and second-year course assignments, twenty-two a page for third- and fourth-year assignments, twenty-four for "technical, scientific, and advanced" topics. "Technical, scientific, and advanced" can mean nuclear physics, as it does in September when there is no business. Or it can mean anything Matthew and Sylvia want it to, as it does in March. Most major spring-term essays are due when final exams begin, in April, and so in March kids are practically lined up in the office taking numbers and spilling out into the hall. The writers get half, in cash: ten and eleven bucks a page; twelve for the technical, scientific, and advanced

There's one other charge: if the client doesn't bring in her or his own books, except in September and January, she or he is "dinged," charged an extra two dollars a page for research. When the writers get an assignment, we ask if there are books. If there are, it saves us time, but we have to lug them home, and often they're the wrong books. If there are no books, we have to go to the libraries and research the paper ourselves. "Client wants twelve pages on clinical social work intervention," Matthew and Sylvia might tell us. "She has a reading list but no books. I think we can ding her." "He wants a book report on something called *Gravity's Rainbow*? Doesn't have the book, though. I'm gonna ding him."

OCTOBER 13. I am assigned a paper on the French philosopher Michel Foucault. The client has been dinged; I have to find some books. Foucault's *Discipline and Punish* and *Madness and Civilization* are hot properties in the public library system. They are not to be found anywhere. Perhaps this is because professors think Foucault is a hot property, too; he's all over everyone's syllabus.

I warn the client about this in the office. "If you don't find anything by the guy, call me," he says. He gives me his home phone number. "Only, *please* don't say you're from the essay service. Say you're . . . a classmate of mine." I promise to be discreet. Most of the clients get scared when you call them at home; most never give out their numbers. I don't blame them.

It was different, though, when I was a university student in the early 1980s. I wasn't aware of anyone who bought his or her homework anywhere, although it must have happened. It was about that time that Tailormade was putting up signs on the telephone poles outside the university's main classroom buildings. It advertised just outside the huge central library as well as outside the libraries of three or four smaller schools a few minutes' drive away. This burst of entrepreneurial confidence almost led to the service's undoing. In a spectacular cooperative sting operation among the security departments of the various schools, the office was raided. This event has become a sort of fearsome myth at Tailormade, discussed not unlike the way Syrians might occasionally mention the Israeli raid on Entebbe. Matthew and Sylvia were hauled off to court and a dozen or so clients were thrown out of their respective universities. Matthew and Sylvia, however, must have hired the right lawyer: they were allowed to reopen, provided that they stayed away from campuses and that they stamped every page of every essay TAILORMADE ESSAY SERVICE: FOR RESEARCH PURPOSES ONLY. Now the clients take the stamped essays home, retype them, and print them out on high-end laser printers much better than ours. If the client is obnoxious, complains, or is considered a whiner, each typewritten page will be stamped in the middle. If the client is steady and has good credit, each page will be stamped in the margin so that the stamp can be whited out and the pages photocopied.

By the time Tailormade reopened, I had moved back to this country after some years at home in the States. I had no money and no prospects of a legal job. I came in, handed Matthew a resume, spent a couple of weeks on probationary trial, and then began a serious career as a hack. "What are your specialties?" Matthew had asked me. I told him I'd majored in history and political science as an undergraduate. Over time, as my financial situation grew worse, my "specialties" grew to include everything except math, accounting, economics, and the hard sciences.

OCTOBER 23. Three weeks ago I was assigned an essay on the establishment and growth of political action committees among the Christian right.

I am earnest about this one; I actually overprepare. I want to document, with carefully muted horror, the world of Paul Laxalt and direct mail, the armtwisting of members of Congress on the school prayer issue. My contempt for the client was mixed with pity: he knew not how much he was missing. Only afterward do I realize that after doing an essay I take seriously, I still expect, as in college, to get something back with a mark on it, as a reward or at least as an acknowledgment. I hear nothing, of course. I feel oddly let down. I'm certain it got the client an A. Today, the same client stops in to order something else and helpfully points out what he thinks I could have done to improve the essay I'd written for him.

OCTOBER 25. This summer, a woman wanted me to write about how aboriginal peoples' systems of law and justice were better developed than those of conquering colonials. I took books with titles like *The Treaties of Canada with the Indians of Manitoba and the North-West Territories*, 1880 to the beach. After finishing the client's reading material, I still had no idea what aboriginal peoples thought about law or anything else; she had given me only books about the conquering colonials. So the paper went on, for twenty-odd pages, about the conquering colonials. Now she wants me to rewrite it. The time I will spend on this second version waters my pay down to about a dollar an hour.

NOVEMBER 8. I will not go into any of the university's libraries. I will not risk running into anyone I know, anyone who might think I'm one of those perpetual graduate students who never finished their dissertations and drift pathetically around university libraries like the undead, frightening the undergraduates. It would be as bad to be thought one of these lifelong grad students as to be suspected of being what I am. So I use the public libraries, usually the one closest to my apartment, on my street corner. It's a community library, with three wonderful librarians, three daily newspapers, and remarkably few books. If I haven't been given the books already, if the client has been dinged and I have to do research on my own, I come here. I have my favorite chair. The librarians assume I am a "mature" and "continuing" community college student, and make kind chitchat with me.

Sometimes, when I can't find any of the sources listed in the library's computer and don't have time to go to a real library, I use books barely appropriate for the essay: books for "young adults," which means twelve-year-olds, or books I have lying around my apartment—like Jane Jacob's *The Death and Life of Great American Cities*, H. D. F. Kitto's *The Greeks*, Eduardo Galeano's *Open Veins of Latin America*, Roy Medvedev's book on Stalin or T. H. White's on John Kennedy, books by J. K. Galbraith, Lewis Mumford, Christopher Lasch, Erich Fromm. Books somewhere between the classic and the old chestnut; terrific books, yet with no relation to the topic at hand. But they're good for the odd quote and name-drop, and they can pad a bibliography. Sometimes I can't get away with this, though, and then I have no choice but to go back to an actual place of research, like the archives.

The archives are, in fact, a difficult place for me. They are full of oak tables, clicking laptops, whirring microfiche readers, and self-assured middle-aged men working with pretty young women whose hair is pinned up in nineteenth-century styles. Perhaps some of them are lovers, but certainly all of them are graduate students with their profs. I, by contrast, am a virtual student, a simulacrum.

NOVEMBER 16. I have also been pulling at least one or two all-nighters a week for three weeks now. They're very much like the all-nighters I did as an undergraduate. I eat licorice nibs for energy and drink molehill coffee for caffeine. You make molehill coffee by pouring an entire half cup of coffee grounds, the finer the better, in a number 4 paper filter, one filter per cup. At midnight the razzy voice of Tom Waits is temporarily replaced by the BBC news hour. It would be great to be able to speak just like the BBC newscaster. Somebody hyphen-Jones. If I sounded like that I'm sure I would be able to get credit, somehow, for writing about the birth of the Carolingian Renaissance, or the displacement of the samurai in Tokugawa times, or the inadequacies of the Treaty of Versailles.

I know by experience that if I start writing at midnight I can time my output: first page by the BBC's second news summary, second page by the financial news on the half hour, third page finished by the time they read the rugby scores. Except that the first page, the one with the thesis paragraph in it, is the hardest to write, and it clocks in at well over fifteen minutes.

At two-thirty I hit a wall. The molehill coffee still hasn't kicked in yet, or else it did and I didn't notice, and now it's worn off, or else I've just built up a fatal tolerance to the stuff, like a crack addict. I begin to fall asleep in my chair, even with my headphones on. I turn up the music and blast it through the headphones. This works for the time being. I plug along. I can't really remember what I said in my thesis paragraph, but I am not going to worry about it. The client wants fifteen pages, and when I find myself on the fourteenth I'11 read the thing over and brace myself, if I have to, for a bow-out. Bow-outs, like legal fine print, allow you to dart gracefully out of the large ambitious thesis statement you've started the essay with: "The topic of bird evolution is an enormous one; I have been able to touch on just one or two interesting controversies within it." "Space does not permit a detailed discussion of all the internal contradictions within Sri Lanka's postcolonial history." And so on. Nine and a half pages down. Five and a half to go. I can still barely remember what I said in my thesis statement. I can barely remember what this paper is *about*. I want to put my head down for a minute on the keyboard, but God only knows what it would end up typing.

NOVEMBER 18. Things are picking up for Christmas vacation; everything, it seems, is due December 5 or December 15. The essay order form asks, "Subject & Level," "Topic," "No. of Pages," "Footnotes," "Bibliography," and then a couple of lines marked "Additional Information," by far the most common of which is "Simple English." As the year rolls on, we hacks will all, out of annoyance, laziness, or just boredom, start unsimplifying this simple English; by April it will approach the mega-watt vocabulary and tortured syntax of the Frankfurt School. But people hand these papers in and don't get caught, people who have difficulty speaking complete sentences in English; perhaps this is because classes and even tutorials are so big they never have to speak. But in December we're all still on pretty good behavior, simple instead of spiteful. I've just handed in an assignment in "Simple English," a paper titled "Mozart's Friendship with Joseph and Johann Michael Haydn and Its Impact on Mozart's Chamber Music." It reads, in part:

Mozart was undeniably original. He was never derivative. That was part of his genius. So were the Haydn brothers. All of them were totally unique.

The little library on my corner didn't have much on Mozart or the Haydn brothers. As a result, one of the items in my bibliography is a child's book with a cardboard pop-up of a doughy-looking little Mozart, in a funky pigtail and knee breeches, standing proudly beside a harpsichord.

NOVEMBER 22. I'm assigned an overnight rush essay on the causes of the English Civil War. It may sound perverse, but I love rush essays. We get paid a dollar more a page (two for technical, scientific, and advanced), and if it's lousy we can always say, "Well, you wanted it in a hurry." Although I majored in history, I never took any courses on the English Civil War; I figured, wrongly, that Shakespeare's histories would take care of that. Now I find myself reading the books I took out from the little corner library, not for quotes, or to form an opinion on the roots, germination, feeding, and watering of the war, but just to find out what the hell went on. I find out enough to write five pages. It takes me all night.

NOVEMBER 23. I am handing in something entitled "Sri Lanka: A Study in Ethnic Division and Caste Co-optation," which Sylvia assigned me, over the phone, a week ago. "The girl says to tell you that *she's* Sri Lankan." Last year I wrote a senior sociology thesis on "The Italian-Canadian Family: Bedrock of Tradition or Agent of Change?" With that one I heard, "The girl says to tell you that *she's* Italian." I wanted to ask Sylvia if the client knew I wasn't, but I was afraid she'd interpret that as meaning I didn't want the work and she'd give it to someone else.

DECEMBER 2. Occasionally there is an assignment the writers fight for. This week somebody—not me—gets to take home *Fanny Hill* and *Lady Chatterley's Lover*, and get paid for it. I guess some kids really, *really* hate to read.

DECEMBER 5. A bad assignment: unnecessarily obscure, pedantic, pointless. Certain courses seem to consist of teaching kids the use of jargon as though it were a substitute for writing or thinking well. Often there is an implied pressure to agree with the assigned book. And many are simply impossible to understand; I often take home a textbook or a sheaf of photocopies for an assignment and see, next to a phrase such as "responsible acceptance of the control dimension," long strings of tiny Chinese characters in ballpoint pen. No wonder the students find the assignments incomprehensible; they are incomprehensible to me.

DECEMBER 8. I hand in a paper on Machiavelli. "How'd it go?" asked the client, a boy in a leather bomber jacket reading John Grisham. I begin to go on about how great one of the books was, a revisionist biography called *Machiavelli in Hell*. I am hoping, with my scholarly enthusiasm, to make the client feel particularly stupid. "It's an amazing book," I tell him. "It makes a case for Machiavelli actually being kind of a liberal humanist instead of the cynical guy everybody always thinks he was—amazing." "That's good," the kid says. "I'm glad you're enjoying yourself on my tab. Did you answer the essay question the way you were supposed to?"

DECEMBER 16. Every so often clients come in with an opinion they want us to replicate. The freshman sociology and political science essays are already starting to rain in: a deluge of "Show why immigrants are a dead weight on the economy and take jobs away from us"; "Show why most social programs will become too expensive for an aging population"; "Show why gun control can be interpreted as an infringement on civil rights"; "Show the Pacific Rim's single-handed assault on North American economies." I ignore them. I write, depending on my mood, about the INS's unequal criteria for refugee status, or the movie *Roger and Me*, or the NRA's political clout. For instance, there is today's assignment: to describe Locke's influence, as an Enlightenment figure, on our own time. I think this is baloney. I talk about how the postwar military-industrial complex proves that God really did give the world, whatever Locke thought, to the covetous and contentious instead of to the industrious and the rational. No one's ever complained about finding my opinion in a paper instead of their own. Now I realize this isn't because I've persuaded anybody of anything. It's just laziness: there are some customers who actually retype their stamped essays without bothering to read them.

DECEMBER 27. During Christmas vacation, friends of mine invite me to a party. Some people will be there whom we know from college; they are in the process of becoming successful, even making it big. It will be important to project confidence, the illusion of fulfilling my abandoned early promise. "What do I say," I ask my friends, "when somebody asks me what I do for a living?"

"Tell them you're a writer."

My friend Lisa sticks by me loyally all evening. When people ask me, "What is it you do?" Lisa answers for me quickly: "She's a writer."

"Oh, what is it you write?"

"*Essays,*" I say, spitefully, drunkenly. Lisa thinks fast.

"Articles," she says. "She writes articles, on Sri Lanka, and Machiavelli, and the English Civil War."

"Isn't *that* interesting," they say, leaving us for the guacamole.

JANUARY 10, 1995. School has been back in session for a week now. The only work that is in are essays from the education students. I have these assignments. I have trouble manipulating the self-encapsulated second language in which teaching students seem compelled to write. But it's after Christmas, and I'm broke. Education assignments all involve writing up our customers' encounters in their "practicum." Teaching students work several times a week as assistant teachers in grade school classrooms; instead of getting paid for this work, they pay tuition for it. Unfortunately, these expensive practice sessions don't seem to go well. My first such assignment was to write "reflections" on a "lesson plan" for a seventh-grade English class. The teaching student had given me some notes, and I had to translate these into the pedagogical jargon used in her textbooks. The idea seems to be that you have to say, as obscurely as possible, what you did with your seventh-grade kids and what you think about what you did:

Preliminary Lesson Formulations: My objectives were to integrate lesson content with methodology to expand students' receptiveness and responsiveness to the material and to one another by teaching them how to disagree with one another in a constructive way. The class will draw up a T-chart covering "Disagreeing in an Agreeable Way," roughly in the manner of Bennett et al. Check for understanding. When the students discuss this, they are encouraged to listen to one another's language carefully and "correct" it if the wording is unhelpful, negative, or destructive. I shared my objectives with the class by asking them to read a fable and then divide into pairs and decide together what the moral was. Clearly, this is the "Think-Pair-Share" technique, as detailed in Bennett et al. The three strategies in use, then, are: 1) pair and sharing; 2) group discussion of the fable with mind-mapping; 3) group discussion of ways of disagreement. The teacher, modeling, divides the board in two with a line.

"Pair and share" seemed to mean "find a partner." I had no idea what "mind-mapping" or a "T-chart" was supposed to be. And come to think of it, after reading the fable, I had no idea what the moral was.

JANUARY 18. Somebody is applying to the graduate program in family therapy at some university somewhere and wants us to write the application. "She's my friend," said the young woman sitting across from Matthew at the desk. "She wants to start her own private practice as a therapist, right So she can buy a house, right? And if you're a psychiatrist you have to go all the way through med school, right? So she's given me some notes for you about her here—she only needs one credit for her B.A. in psychology, and she volunteered at a shelter one summer. She wants you to tell them all that. Maybe make up some other things."

"See," Matthew tells me after she leaves. "If you ever go to one of those therapists, that's something you should think about."

JANUARY 20. When I first started this work, friends of mine would try to comfort me by telling me it would teach me to write better. Actually, academic prostitution, just like any other kind, seems to bring with it diseases, afflictions, vices, and bad habits. There is, for instance, the art of pretending you've read a book you haven't. It's just like every speed-reading course ever offered by the Learning Annex: read the introduction, where the writer outlines what he's going to say, and the conclusion, where he repeats what he's said.

> In his book *The Technological Society*, Jacques Ellul begins by defining the technical simply as the search for efficiency. He claims, however, that technique itself is subdivided into three categories: the social, the organizational, and the economic.

This is all on the book's *first four pages*. Sometimes—often—I find myself eating up as much space as possible. There are several ways to do this. One is to reproduce lengthy, paragraph-long quotes in full; another is to ramble on about your own apparently passionate opinion on something. Or you start talking about the United States and what a handbasket it's going to hell in. This is equally useful, for different reasons, on either side of the border. You can ask rhetorical questions to obsessive excess. ("Can Ellul present the technical in such a reductionist way? Can he really define technique in such a way? And is it really valid to distinguish between the social and the organizational?" etc.) And there's always the art of name-dropping as a way to fill pages and convince the teaching assistant that your client has read *something*, even if it wasn't what was on the syllabus.

> Certainly, as writers from Eduardo Galeano to Andre Gunder Frank to Noam Chomsky to Philip Agee to Allan Frankovich to Ernesto Laclau document, the CIA has long propped up the United Fruit Company.

At least you can make the client feel stupid. It's the third week of January, my apartment is cold, and I am bitter.

FEBRUARY 8. I'm learning, as the environmentalists tell us, to reuse and recycle. It's easier when I adapt a paper, with minor changes, on the same topic for different classes, or when I use the same paper for the same class again the following year. I've never worried much about a recycled essay being recognized: the pay for teaching assistants is low enough, and the burnout rate high enough, that the odds are substantially against the same person reading and grading papers for the same course two years in a row. Some topics just seem to beg for recycling: freshmen are forever being asked to mull over the roles of determinism, hubris, and moral responsibility in the Oedipus cycle; sociology and philosophy majors, the ethics of abortion. There are essays on shantytowns in developing countries, export-oriented economies in developing countries, structural adjustment in developing countries, and one only has to make the obvious case that the three are interrelated to be able to extend the possibilities for parts of essays in any of those three categories to resurface magically within another. Other essays can be recycled with just a little tinkering to surmount minor differences in topic or in emphasis: for instance, "Italian Fascists in North America," to which "The Italian-Canadian Family" lends itself nicely; "Taboo-Breaking in Racine and Ford," which re-emerges, after minor cosmetic surgery, as "Master-Slave Relationships in Ford and Racine: What They Tell Us About Lust, Fate, and Obligation." And so on.

FEBRUARY 15. I'm sitting on the floor with a pile of old magazines, cutting out pictures of Oreo cookies and Wendy's burgers. This is Andy's essay. It's not an essay, actually, it's a food bingo chart. I have to find a large sheet of cardboard, divide it into squares, and glue on pictures of what is recognizably food. Andy is another education student: he wants to teach junior kindergarten, and his assignment is, apparently, to teach the little tots where food comes from, or what it is, or that advertising is a vital component of each of the four basic food groups, or something. I come into Tailormade with food bingo under my arm. I've gotten some strange looks on the subway. It nets me twenty-five bucks.

MARCH 7. I was supposed to turn in an essay today, one I don't have. I fell asleep at the keyboard last night and accidentally slept through the whole night, headphones and all.

MARCH 16. There's a regular customer whose course load would be appropriate for the resume of a U.N. secretary general. She's taking several courses on developing economies, including one referred to by other clients in the same class as "Third World Women." And one on the history of black Americans from Reconstruction to the present. I wrote her a twenty-five-page history of the early years of the civil-rights movement. She was sitting in the office when I handed it in. "Interesting course, isn't it?" she asked. She requested me again. I wrote her a paper on Costa Rica, one on dowry murders in India, one on the black leader W. E. B. Du Bois. "It's a great course, isn't it?" she asked me when she got the paper on dowry murders. "He seems like a fascinating guy," she said the day she collected W. E. B. Du Bois. "Somebody told me he wound up in *Ghana*." Today I take a short-cut across the university campus on my way to the essay service and see her with a group of other students. I make a direct beeline for her and I smile. I watch her blanch, look around, try to decide whether to pretend not to know me, decide that maybe that isn't a good idea. She gives me a stricken look and a big toothy grin.

MARCH 26. One day I'm given five pages on the Treaty of Versailles. Last year at the same time, I was assigned a paper on the same topic. A memorable paper. Two days after I turned it in, there was a camera crew outside. It turned out to be the local cable station for kids, doing an "exposé" on cheating. We taped it when it came on. It featured kids sitting in shadow, faces obscured, *60 Minutes* style.

"There she is, the little rat," Sylvia glowered at the time. The pretty young fake client handed my paper to some professor sitting behind a desk and asked, "What do you think about this? Is it better or worse than what you would normally get? Would you assume that it was a real paper or one that had been bought?"

"Well . . . it's a *credible* paper," said the professor. "I mean, one wouldn't think it was . . . *synthetic* unless one had reason to."

"What kind of grade would you give it?"

"Oh, I'd give it. . . a B minus."

"*Please.*" I was really offended. Elliott comforted me. "Well, he has to say that. Now that he knows it's ours, he can't admit it's an A paper even if he wants to."

We all sat tight and waited for every professor within fifty miles to call us, threatening death. But professors don't watch cable shows for teenagers; neither do ambitious young teaching assistants. Instead, the show turned out to be a free advertising bonanza. Soon the phone rang off the hook with kids calling up and asking, "You mean, like, you can write my term paper for me if I pay you?"

APRIL 16. Today, working on a paper, I was reminded that there are good professors. They're the ones who either convince the kids the course content is inherently interesting and get them to work hard on the assignments or who figure out ways to make the assignments, at least, creative events to enjoy. But students with shaky language skills falter at surprises, even good ones; lazy students farm the assignments out no matter what they are. Such assignments are oddly comforting for me: I can almost pretend the two of us are talking over the clients' heads. When I'm alone in my room, in front of the computer and between the headphones, it's hard not to want to write something good for myself and maybe even for the imaginary absentee professor or appreciative T.A., something that will last. But when I'm standing in the crowded Tailormade office, next to someone elegant and young and in eight hundred bucks' worth of calfskin leather, someone who not only has never heard of John Stuart Mill and never read Othello but doesn't even know he hasn't, doesn't even mind that he hasn't, and doesn't even care that he hasn't, the urge to make something that will last somehow vanishes.

APRIL 28. The semester is almost at an end. Exams have started; the essays have all been handed in. Elliott and Russell begin their summer jobs as bike couriers. Henry, like me, is illegal; but he confides to me that he's had enough. "You can only do so much of this," he says. I know, I tell him. I know.

PEGGY R. SANDAY

PULLING TRAIN

T his article discusses certain group rituals of male bonding on a college campus, in particular, a phenomenon called "pulling train." According to a report issued by the Association of American Colleges in 1985, "pulling train," or "gang banging" as it is also called, refers to a group of men lining up like train cars to take turns having sex with the same woman (Ehrhart and Sandler 1985, 2). This report labels "pulling train" as gang rape. Bernice Sandler, one of its authors, recently reported that she had found more than seventy-five documented cases of gang rape on college campuses in recent years (*Atlanta Constitution*, 7 June 1988). Sandler labeled these incidents gang rape because of the coercive nature of the sexual behavior. The incidents she and Julie K. Ehrhart described in their 1985 report display a common pattern. A vulnerable young woman, one who is seeking acceptance or who is high on drugs or alcohol, is taken to a room. She may or may not agree to have sex with one man. She then passes out, or is too weak or scared to protest, and a train of men have sex with her. Sometimes the young woman's drinks are spiked without her knowledge, and when she is approached by several men in a locked room, she reacts with confusion and panic. Whether too weak to protest, frightened, or unconscious, as has been the case in quite a number of instances, anywhere from two to eleven or more men have sex with her. In some party invitations the possibility of such an occurrence is mentioned with playful allusions to "gang bang" or "pulling train" (Ehrhart and Sandler 1985, 1-2). The reported incidents occurred at all kinds of institutions: "public, private, religiously affiliated, Ivy League, large and small" (ibid.). Most of the incidents occurred at fraternity parties, but some occurred in residence halls or in connection with college athletics. Incidents have also been reported in high schools. . . . Just a few examples taken from the Ehrhart and Sandler report (1985, 1-2) are sufficient to demonstrate the coercive nature of the sexual behavior.

> The 17-year-old freshman woman went to the fraternity "little sister" rush party with two of her roommates. The roommates left early without her. She was trying to get a ride home when a fraternity brother told her he would take her home after the party ended. While she waited, two other fraternity members took her into a bedroom to "discuss little sister matters." The door was closed and one of the brothers stood blocking the exit. They told her that in order to become a little sister (honorary member) she would have to have sex with a fraternity member. She was frightened, fearing they would physically harm her if she refused. She could see no escape. Each of the brothers had sex with her, as did a third who had been hiding in the room. During the next two hours a succession of men went into the room. There were never less than three men with her, sometimes more. After they let her go, a fraternity brother drove her home. He told her not to feel bad about the incident because another woman had also been "upstairs" earlier that night. (Large southern university)

> It was her first fraternity party. The beer flowed freely and she had much more to drink than she had planned. It was hot and crowded and the party spread out all over the house, so that when three men asked her to go upstairs, she went with them. They took her into a bedroom, locked the door and began to undress her. Groggy with alcohol, her feeble protests were ignored as the three men raped her. When they finished; they put her in the hallway, naked, locking her clothes in the bedroom. (Small eastern liberal arts college)

A 19-year-old woman student was out on a date with her boyfriend and another couple. They were all drinking beer and after going back to the boyfriend's dorm room, they smoked two marijuana cigarettes. The other couple left and the woman and her boyfriend had sex. The woman fell asleep and the next thing she knew she awoke with a man she didn't know on top of her trying to force her into having sex. A witness said the man was in the hall with two other men when the woman's boyfriend came out of his room and invited them to have sex with his unconscious girlfriend. (Small midwestern college)

Although Ehrhart and Sandler boldly labeled the incidents they described as rape, few of the perpetrators were prosecuted. Generally speaking, the male participants are protected and the victim is blamed for having placed herself in a compromising social situation where male adolescent hormones are known, as the saying goes, "to get out of hand." For a number of reasons, people say, "She asked for it." As the above examples from the Ehrhart and Sandler report suggest, the victim may be a vulnerable young woman who is seeking acceptance or who is weakened by the ingestion of drugs or alcohol. She may or may not agree to having sex with one man. If she has agreed to some sexual activity, the men assume that she has agreed to all sexual activity regardless of whether she is conscious or not. In the minds of the boys involved the sexual behavior is not rape. On many campuses this opinion is shared by a significant portion of the campus community. . . .

THE XYZ EXPRESS

I first learned about "pulling train" in 1983 from a student who was then enrolled in one of my classes. Laurel had been out of class for about two weeks. I noticed her absence and worried that she was getting behind on her work. When she came back to class she told me that she had been raped by five or six male students at a fraternity house after one of the fraternity's weekly Thursday night parties. Later, I learned from others that Laurel was drunk on beer and had taken four hits of LSD before going to the party.

According to the story Laurel told to a campus administrator, after the party she fell asleep in a first-floor room and when she awoke was undressed. One of the brothers dressed her and carried her upstairs, where she was raped by "guys" she did not know but said she could identify if photographs were available. She asked a few times for the men to get off her, but to no avail. According to her account, she was barely conscious and lacked the strength to push them off her.

There is no dispute that Laurel had a serious drinking and drug problem at the time of the party. People at the party told me that during the course of the evening she acted like someone who was "high," and her behavior attracted quite a bit of attention. They described her as dancing provocatively to the beat of music only she could hear. She appeared disoriented and out of touch with what was happening. Various fraternity brothers occasionally danced with her, but she seemed oblivious to the person she was dancing with. Some of the brothers teased her by spinning her around in a room until she was so dizzy she couldn't find her way out. At one point during the evening she fell down a flight of stairs. Later she was pulled by the brothers out of a circle dance, a customary fraternity ritual in which only brothers usually took part.

After the other partyers had gone home, the accounts of what happened next vary according to who tells the story. The differences of opinion do not betray a Rashomon effect as much as they reflect different definitions of a common sexual event. No one disputes that Laurel had sex with at least five or six male students, maybe more. When Anna, a friend of the XYZ brothers, saw Laurel the next day and heard the story from the brothers, her immediate conclusion was that they had raped Laurel. Anna based her conclusion on seeing Laurel's behavior at the party and observing her the following day. It seemed to Anna that Laurel was incapable of consenting to sex, which is key for determining a charge of rape. Anna's opinion was later confirmed by the Assistant District Attorney for Sex Crimes, who investigated but did not prosecute the case.

The brothers claimed that Laurel had lured them into a "gang bang" or "train," which they preferred to call an "express." Their statements and actions during the days after the event seemed to indicate that they considered the event a routine part of their "little sisters program," something to be proud of. Reporting the party activities on a sheet posed on their bulletin board in the spot where the house minutes are usually posted, Anna found the following statement, which she later showed me:

> Things are looking up for the [XYZ] sisters program. A prospective leader for the group spent some time interviewing several [brothers] this past thursday and friday. Possible names for the little sisters include [XYZ] "little wenches" and "The [XYZ] express."

. . . The ideology that promotes "pulling train" is seen in the discourse and practices associated with some parties on campus. Party invitations expressing this ideology depict a woman lying on a pool table, or in some other position suggestive of sexual submission. The hosts of the party promote behavior aimed at seduction. *Seduction* means plying women with alcohol or giving them drugs in order to "break down resistance." A drunken woman is not defined as being in need of protection and help, but as "asking for it." If the situation escalates into sexual activity, the brothers watch each other perform sexual acts and then brag about "getting laid." The event is referred to as "drunken stupidity, women chasing, and all around silliness." The drama enacted parodies the image of the gentleman. Its male participants brag about their masculinity and its female participants are degraded to the status of what the boys call "red meat" or "fish." The whole scenario coins men in a no-holds-barred orgy of togetherness. The woman whose body facilitates all of this is sloughed off at the end like a used condom. She may be called a "nympho" or the men may believe that they seduced her—a practice known as "working a yes out"—through promises of becoming a little sister, by getting her drunk, by promising her love, or by some other means. Those men who object to this kind of behavior run the risk of being labeled "wimps" or, even worse in their eyes, "gays" or "faggots."

The rationalization for this behavior illustrates a broader social ideology of male dominance. Both the brothers and many members of the broader community excuse the behavior by saying that "boys will be boys" and that if a woman gets into trouble it is because "she asked for it," "she wanted it," or "she deserved it." The ideology inscribed in this discourse represents male sexuality as more natural and more explosive than female sexuality. This active, "naturally" explosive nature of male sexuality is expected to find an outlet either in the company of male friends or in the arms of prostitutes. In these contexts men are supposed to use women to satisfy explosive urges. The women who satisfy these urges are included as passive actors in the enactment of a sexual discourse where the male, but not the female, sexual instinct is characterized as an insatiable biological instinct and psychological need.

Men entice one another into the act of "pulling train" by implying that those who do not participate are unmanly or homosexual. This behavior is full of contradictions because the homoeroticism of "pulling train" seems obvious. A group of men watch each other having sex with a woman who may be unconscious. One might well ask why the woman is even necessary for the sexual acts these men stage for one another. As fraternity practices described in this book suggest, the answer seems to lie in homophobia. One can suggest that in the act of "pulling train" the polymorphous sexuality of homophobic men is given a strictly heterosexual form.

Polymorphous sexuality, a term used by Freud to refer to diffuse sexual interests with multiple objects, means that men will experience desire for one another. However, homophobia creates a tension between polymorphous sexual desire and compulsory heterosexuality. This tension is resolved by "pulling train": the brothers vent their interest in one another through the body of a woman. In the sociodrama that is enacted, the idea that heterosexual males are superior to women and to homosexuals is publicly expressed and probably subjectively absorbed. Thus, both homophobia and compulsory heterosexuality can be understood as strategies of knowledge and power centering on sex that support the social stratification of men according to sexual preference.

In group sex, homoerotic desire is simultaneously indulged, degraded, and extruded from the group. The fact that the woman involved is often unconscious highlights her status as a surrogate victim in a drama where the main agents are males interacting with one another. The victim embodies the sexual urges of the brothers; she is defined as "wanting it"—even though she may be unconscious during the event—so that the men can satisfy their urges for one another at her expense. By defining the victim as "wanting it," the men convince themselves of their heterosexual prowess and delude themselves as to the real object of their lust. If they were to admit to the real object, they would give up their position in the male status hierarchy as superior, heterosexual males. The expulsion and degradation of the victim both brings a momentary end to urges that would divide the men and presents a social statement of phallic heterosexual dominance.

By blaming the victim for provoking their own sexual aggression, men control and define acceptable and unacceptable female sexual behavior through the agency of fear. The fear is that a woman who does not guard her behavior runs the risk of becoming the target of uncontrollable male sexual aggression. Thus, although women are ostensibly the controlling agent, it is fear of the imagined explosive nature of male sexuality that ultimately reigns for both sexes. This fear instills in some men and women consciousness of their sexual and social identities.

In sum, the phenomenon of "pulling train" has many meanings. In addition to those meanings that have been mentioned, it is a bonding device that can permanently change a young man's understanding of masculinity. The bonding is accomplished by virtue of coparticipation in a "forbidden" act. As Ward Goodenough (1963) points out, sharing in the forbidden as part of initiation to a group is a powerful bonding device. For example, criminal gangs may require the initiate to perform a criminal act in order to be accepted as a member, an act that once performed is irrevocable. Participation in a "train" performs the same function of bonding the individual to the group and changing his subjectivity. Such bridge-burning acts of one kind or another are standard parts of ritualized identity-change procedures.

THE CONDITIONS PROMOTING "PULLING TRAIN"

We cannot assume that all entering college students have well-established sexual and social identities or ethical positions regarding sexual harassment and abuse. Recent research by psychologists on human subjectivity argues that subjectivity is dynamic and changes as individuals move through the life cycle. The evidence presented here suggests that the masculine subjectivity of insecure males may be shaped, or at least reinforced, by experiences associated with male bonding at college.

[One] example is fraternity initiation rituals in which young men who admit to feelings of low self-esteem upon entering the college setting are forced to cleanse and purify themselves of the despised and dirty feminine, "nerdy," "faggot" self bonded to their mothers. The ritual process in these cases humiliates the pledges in order to break social and psychological bonds to parental authority and to establish new bonds to the brotherhood. The traumatic means employed to achieve these goals induces a state of consciousness that makes abuse of women a means to renew fraternal bonds and assert power as a brotherhood. . . .

. . . Cross-cultural research demonstrates that whenever men build and give allegiance to a mystical, enduring, all-male social group, the disparagement of women is, invariably, an important ingredient of the mystical bond, and sexual aggression the means by which the bond is renewed (Sanday 1981, 1986). As long as exclusive male clubs exist in a society that privileges men as a social category, we must recognize that collective sexual aggression provides a ready stage on which some men represent their social privilege and introduce adolescent boys to their future place in the status hierarchy.

Why has the sexual abuse of women and the humiliation of generations of pledges been tolerated for so long? The answer lies in a historical tendency to privilege male college students by failing to hold them accountable. Administrators protect young men by dissociating asocial behavior from the perpetrator and attributing it to something else. For example, one hears adult officials complaining about violence committed by fraternity brothers at the same time they condone the violence by saying that "things got out of hand" because of alcohol, adolescence, or some other version of "boys will be boys." Refusing to take serious action against young offenders promotes the male privilege that led to the behavior in the first place. At some level, perhaps, administrators believe that by taking effective action to end all forms of abuse they deny young men a forum for training for masculinity. Where this is the case women students cannot possibly experience the same social opportunities or sense of belonging at college as their male peers, even though they spend the same amount of money for the privilege of attending. As colleges and universities face an increasing number of legal suits deriving from rape, murder, and the other forms of abuse reported in fraternities, athletic settings, and dorms, change is clearly imminent. . . .

REFERENCES

Ehrhart, Julie K., and Bernice R. Sandler. 1985. "Campus Gang Rape: Party Games?" Washington, D.C.: Project on the Status of Women, Association of American Colleges.

Goodenough, Ward Hunt. 1963. *Cooperation in Change.* New York: Russell Sage Foundation.

Sanday, Peggy Reeves. 1981. "The Socio-Cultural Context of Rape." *Journal of Social Issues* 37: 5-27.

_____. 1986. "Rape and the Silencing of the Feminine." In *Rape: A Collection of Essays,* edited by Roy Porter and Sylvana Tomaselli. London: Basil Blackwell.

COLLEGE SUBJECTS

LEWIS THOMAS

THE ART OF TEACHING SCIENCE

Everyone seems to agree that there is something wrong with the way science is being taught these days. But no one is at all clear about when it went wrong or what is to be done about it. The term "scientific illiteracy" has become almost a cliché in educational circles. Graduate schools blame the colleges; colleges blame the secondary schools; the high schools blame the elementary schools, which, in turn, blame the family.

I suggest that the scientific community itself is partly, perhaps largely, to blame. Moreover, if there are disagreements between the world of the humanities and the scientific enterprise as to the place and importance of science in a liberal-arts education and the role of science in 20th-century culture, I believe that the scientists are themselves responsible for a general misunderstanding of what they are really up to.

During the last half-century, we have been teaching the sciences as though they were the same collection of academic subjects as always, and—here is what has really gone wrong—as though they would always be the same. Students learn today's biology, for example, the same way we learned Latin when I was in high school long ago: first, the fundamentals; then, the underlying laws; next, the essential grammar and, finally, the reading of texts. Once mastered, that was that: Latin was Latin and forever after would always be Latin. History, once learned, was history. And biology was precisely biology, a vast array of hard facts to be learned as fundamentals, followed by a reading of the texts.

From *The New York Times Magazine*, 1982. Reprinted by permission of *The New York Times*.

Furthermore, we have been teaching science as if its facts were somehow superior to the facts in all other scholarly disciplines—more fundamental. more solid, less subject to subjectivism, immutable. English literature is not just one way of thinking; it is all sorts of ways; poetry is a moving target; the facts that underlie art, architecture and music are not really hard facts, and you can change them any way you like by arguing about them. But science, it appears, is an altogether different kind of learning: an unambiguous, unalterable and endlessly useful display of data that only needs to be packaged and installed somewhere in one's temporal lobe in order to achieve a full understanding of the natural world.

And, of course, it is not like this at all. In real life, every field of science is incomplete, and most of them—whatever the record of accomplishment during the last 200 years—are still in their very earliest stages. In the fields I know best among the life sciences, it is required that the most expert and sophisticated minds be capable of changing course—often with a great lurch every few years. In some branches of biology the mind-changing is occurring with accelerating velocity. Next week's issue of any scientific journal can turn a whole field upside down, shaking out any number of immutable ideas and installing new bodies of dogma. This is an almost everyday event in physics, in chemistry, in materials research, in neurobiology, in genetics, in immunology.

On any Tuesday morning, if asked, a good working scientist will tell you with some self-satisfaction that the affairs of his field are nicely in order, that things are finally looking clear and making sense, and all is well. But come back again on another Tuesday, and the roof may have just fallen in on his life's work. All the old ideas—last week's ideas in some cases—are no longer good ideas. The hard facts have softened, melted away and vanished under the pressure of new hard facts. Something strange has happened. And it is this very strangeness of nature that makes science engrossing, that keeps bright people at it, and that ought to be at the center of science teaching.

The conclusions reached in science are always, when looked at closely, far more provisional and tentative than are most of the assumptions arrived at by our colleagues in the humanities. But we do not talk much in public about this, nor do we teach this side of science. We tend to say instead:

These are the facts of the matter, and this is what the facts signify. Go and learn them, for they will be the same forever.

By doing this, we miss opportunity after opportunity to recruit young people into science, and we turn off a good many others who would never dream of scientific careers but who emerge from their education with the impression that science is fundamentally boring.

Sooner or later, we will have to change this way of presenting science. We might begin by looking more closely at the common ground that science shares with all disciplines, particularly with the humanities and with social and behavioral science. For there is indeed such a common ground. It is called bewilderment. There are more than seven times seven types of ambiguity in science, all awaiting analysis. The poetry of Wallace Stevens is crystal clear alongside the genetic code.

One of the complaints about science is that it tends to flatten everything. In its deeply reductionist way, it is said, science removes one mystery after another, leaving nothing in the place of mystery but data. I have even heard this claim as explanation for the drift of things in modern art and modern music: Nothing is left to contemplate except randomness and senselessness; God is nothing but a pair of dice, loaded at that. Science is linked somehow to the despair of the 20th-century mind. There is almost nothing unknown and surely nothing unknowable. Blame science.

I prefer to turn things around in order to make precisely the opposite case. Science, especially 20th-century science, has provided us with a glimpse of something we never really knew before, the revelation of human ignorance. We have been accustomed to the belief, from one century to another, that except for one or two mysteries we more or less comprehend everything on earth. Every age, not just the 18th century, regarded itself as the Age of Reason, and we have never lacked for explanations of the world and its ways. Now, we are being brought up short. We do not understand much of anything, from the episode we rather dismissively (and, I think, defensively) choose to call the "big bang," all the way down to the particles in the atoms of a bacterial cell. We have a wilderness of mystery to make our way through in the centuries ahead. We will need science for this but not science alone. In its own time, science will produce the data and some of the meaning in the data, but never the full meaning. For perceiving real significance when significance is at hand, we will need all sorts of brains outside the fields of science.

It is primarily because of this need that I would press for changes in the way science is taught. Although there is a perennial need to teach the young people who will be doing the science themselves, this will always be a small minority. Even more important, we must teach science to those who will be needed for thinking about it, and that means pretty nearly everyone else— most of all, the poets, but also artists, musicians, philosophers, historians and writers. A few of these people, at least, will be able to imagine new levels of meaning which may be lost on the rest of us.

In addition, it is time to develop a new group of professional thinkers, perhaps a somewhat larger group than the working scientists and the working poets, who can create a discipline of scientific criticism. We have had good luck so far in the emergence of a few people ranking as philosophers of science and historians and journalists of science, and I hope more of these will be coming along. But we have not yet seen specialists in the fields of scientific criticism who are of the caliber of the English literary and social critics F. R. Leavis and John Ruskin or the American literary critic Edmund Wilson. Science needs critics of this sort, but the public at large needs them more urgently.

I suggest that the introductory courses in science, at all levels from grade school through college, be radically revised. Leave the fundamentals, the so-called basics, aside for a while, and concentrate the attention of all students on the things that are not known. You cannot possibly teach quantum mechanics without mathematics, to be sure, but you can describe the strangeness of the world opened up by quantum theory. Let it be known, early on, that there are deep mysteries and profound paradoxes revealed in distant outline by modern physics. Explain that these can be approached more closely and puzzled over, once the language of mathematics has been sufficiently mastered.

At the outset, before any of the fundamentals, teach the still imponderable puzzles of cosmology. Describe as clearly as possible, for the youngest minds, that there are some things going on in the universe that lie still beyond comprehension, and make it plain how little is known.

Do not teach that biology is a useful and perhaps profitable science; that can come later. Teach instead that there are structures squirming inside each of our cells that provide all the energy for living. Essentially foreign creatures, these lineal descendants of bacteria were brought in for symbiotic living a billion or so years ago. Teach that we do not have the ghost of an idea how they got there, where they came from, or how they evolved to their present structure and function. The details of oxidative phosphorylation and photosynthesis can come later.

Teach ecology early on. Let it be understood that the earth's life is a system of interdependent creatures, and that we do not understand at all how it works. The earth's environment, from the range of atmospheric gases to the chemical constituents of the sea, has been held in an almost unbelievably improbable state of regulated balance since life began, and the regulation of stability and balance is somehow accomplished by the life itself like the autonomic nervous system of an immense organism. We do not know how such a system works, much less what it means, but there are some nice reductionist details at hand, such as the bizarre proportions of atmospheric constituents, ideal for our sort of planetary life, and the surprising stability of the ocean's salinity, and the fact that the average temperature of the earth has remained quite steady in the face of at least a 25 percent increase in heat coming in from the sun since the earth began. That kind of thing: something to think about.

Go easy, I suggest, on the promises sometimes freely offered by science. Technology relies and depends on science these days, more than ever before, but technology is far from the first justification for doing research, nor is it necessarily an essential product to be expected from science. Public decisions about the future of technology are totally different from decisions about science, and the two enterprises should not be tangled together. The central task of science is to arrive, stage by stage, at a clearer comprehension of nature, but this does not at all mean, as it is sometimes claimed to mean, a search for mastery over nature.

Science may someday provide us with a better understanding of ourselves, but never, I hope, with a set of technologies for doing something or other to improve ourselves. I am made nervous by assertions that human consciousness will someday be unraveled by research, laid out for close scrutiny like the workings of a computer, and then—and *then* . . . ! I hope with some fervor that we can learn a lot more than we now know about the human mind, and I see no reason why this strange puzzle should remain forever and entirely beyond us. But I would be deeply disturbed by any prospect that we might use the new knowledge in order to begin doing something about it—to improve it, say. This is a different matter from searching for information to use against schizophrenia or dementia, where we are badly in need of technologies. Indeed likely one day to be sunk without them. But the ordinary, everyday, more or less normal human mind is too marvelous an instrument ever to be tampered with by anyone, science or no science.

The education of humanists cannot be regarded as complete, or even adequate, without exposure in some depth to where things stand in the various branches of science, particularly, as I have said, in the areas of our ignorance. Physics professors, most of them, look with revulsion on assignments to teach their subject to poets. Biologists, caught up by the enchantment of their new power, armed with flawless instruments to tell the nucleotide sequences of the entire human genome, nearly matching the physicists in the precision of their measurements of living processes, will resist the prospect of broad survey courses; each biology professor will demand that any student in his path master every fine detail within that professor's research program.

The liberal-arts faculties, for their part, will continue to view the scientists with suspicion and apprehension. "What do the scientists want?" asked a Cambridge professor in Francis Cornford's wonderful "Microcosmographia Academica." "Everything that's going," was the quick answer. That was back in 1912, and scientists haven't much changed.

But maybe, just maybe, a new set of courses dealing systematically with ignorance in science will take hold. The scientists might discover in it a new and subversive technique for catching the attention of students driven by curiosity, delighted and surprised to learn that science is exactly as the American scientist and educator Vannevar Bush described it: an "endless frontier." The humanists, for their part, might take considerable satisfaction in watching their scientific colleagues confess openly to not knowing everything about everything. And the poets, on whose shoulders the future rests, might, late nights, thinking things over, begin to see some meanings that elude the rest of us. It is worth a try.

I believe that the worst thing that has happened to science education is that the fun has gone out of it. A great many good students look at it as slogging work to be got through on the way to medical school. Others are turned off by the premedical students themselves, embattled and bleeding for grades and class standing when few recognize science as the high adventure it really is, the wildest of all explorations ever taken by human beings, the chance to glimpse things never seen before, the shrewdest maneuver for discovering how the world works. Instead, baffled early on, they are misled into thinking that bafflement is simply the result of not having learned all the facts. They should be told that everyone else is baffled as well—from the professor in his endowed chair down to the platoons of postdoctoral students in the laboratories all night. Every important scientific advance that has come in looking like an answer has turned, sooner or later—usually sooner—into a question. And the game is just beginning

If more students were aware of this, I think many of them would decide to look more closely and to try and learn more about what is known. That is the time when mathematics will become clearly and unavoidably recognizable as an essential, indispensable instrument for engaging in the game, and that is the time for teaching it. The calamitous loss of applied mathematics from what we might otherwise be calling higher education is a loss caused, at least in part, by insufficient incentives for learning the subject. Left by itself, standing there among curriculum offerings, it is not at all clear to the student what it is to be applied to. And there is all of science, next door, looking like an almost-finished field reserved only for chaps who want to invent or apply new technologies. We have had it wrong, and presented it wrong to class after class for several generations.

An appreciation of what is happening in science today, and how great a distance lies ahead for exploring, ought to be one of the rewards of a liberal-arts education. It ought to be good in itself, not something to be acquired on the way to a professional career but part of the cast of thought needed for getting into the kind of century that is now just down the road. Part of the intellectual equipment of an educated person, however his or her time is to be spent, ought to be a feel for the queernesses of nature, the inexplicable thing, the side of life for which informed bewilderment will be the best way of getting through the day.

EVELYN FOX KELLER

FROM WORKING SCIENTIST TO FEMINIST CRITIC

I begin with three vignettes, all drawn from memory.

1965. In my first few years out of graduate school, I held quite conventional beliefs about science. I believed not only in the possibility of clear and certain knowledge of the world, but also in the uniquely privileged access to this knowledge provided by science in general, and by physics in particular. I believed in the accessibility of an underlying (and unifying) "truth" about the world we live in, and I believed that the laws of physics gave us the closest possible approximation of this truth. In short, I was well trained in both the traditional realist worldviews assumed by virtually all scientists and in the conventional epistemological ordering of the sciences. I had, after all, been trained, first, by theoretical physicists, and later, by molecular biologists. This is not to say that I lived my life according to the teachings of physics (or molecular biology), only that when it came to questions about what "really is," I knew where, and how, to look. Although I had serious conflicts about my own ability to be part of this venture, I fully accepted science, arid scientists, as arbiters of truth. Physics (and physicists) were, of course, the highest arbiters.

Somewhere around this time, I came across the proceedings of the first major conference held in the United States on "Women and the Scientific Professions" (Mattfield and Van Aiken 1965)—a subject of inevitable interest to me. I recall reading in those proceedings an argument for more women in science, made by both Erik Erikson and Bruno Bettelheim, based on the invaluable contributions a "specifically female genius" could make to science.

Although earlier in their contributions both Erikson and Bettelheim had each made a number of eminently reasonable observations and recommendations, I flew to these concluding remarks as if waiting for them, indeed forgetting everything else they had said. From the vantage point I then occupied, my reaction was predictable: To put it quite bluntly, I laughed. Laws of nature are universal—how could they possibly depend on the sex of their discoverers? Obviously, I snickered, these psychoanalysts know little enough about science (and by implication, about truth).

1969. I was living in a suburban California house and found myself with time to think seriously about my own mounting conflicts (as well as those of virtually all my female cohorts) about being a scientist. I had taken a leave to accompany my husband on his sabbatical, remaining at home to care for our two small children. Weekly, I would talk to the colleague I had left back in New York and hear his growing enthusiasm as he reported the spectacular successes he was having in presenting our joint work. In between, I would try to understand why my own enthusiasm was not only not growing, but actually diminishing. How I went about seeking such an understanding is worth noting: What I did was to go to the library to gather data about the fate of women scientists in general—more truthfully, to document my own growing disenchantment (even in the face of manifest success) as part of a more general phenomenon reflecting an underlying misfit between women and science. And I wrote to Erik Erikson for further comment on the alarming (yet somehow satisfying) attrition data I was collecting. In short, only a few years after ridiculing his thoughts on the subject, I was ready to at least entertain if not embrace an argument about women in, or out of, science based on "women's nature." Not once during that entire year did it occur to me that at least part of my disenchantment might be related to the fact that I was in fact not sharing in the *kudos* my colleague was reaping for our joint work.

1974. I had not dropped out of science, but I had moved into interdisciplinary, undergraduate teaching. And I had just finished teaching my first women's studies course when I received an invitation to give a series of "Distinguished Lectures" on my work in mathematical biology at the University of Maryland. It was a great honor, and I wanted to do it, but I had a problem. In my women's studies course, I had yielded to the pressure of my students and colleagues to talk openly about what it had been like, as a woman, to become a scientist. In other words, I had been persuaded to publicly air the exceedingly painful story of the struggle that had actually been—a story I had previously only talked about in private, if at all. The effect of doing this was that I actually came to *see* that story as public, that is, of political significance, rather than as simply private, of merely personal significance. As a result, the prospect of continuing to present myself as a disembodied scientist, of talking about my work as if it had been done in a vacuum, as if the fact of my being a woman was entirely irrelevant, had come to feel actually dishonest.

I resolved the conflict by deciding to present in my last lecture a demographic model of women in science—an excuse to devote the bulk of that lecture to a review of the many barriers that worked against the survival of women as scientists, and to a discussion of possible solutions. I concluded my review with the observation that perhaps the most important barrier to success for women in science derived from the pervasive belief in the intrinsic masculinity of scientific thought. Where, I asked, does such a belief come from? What is it doing in science, reputedly the most objective, neutral, and abstract endeavor we know? And what consequences does that belief have for the actual doing of science?

In 1974 "women in science" was not a proper subject for academic or scientific discussion; I was aware of violating professional protocol. Having given the lecture—having "carried it off"—I felt profoundly liberated. I had passed an essential milestone.

Although I did not know it then, and wouldn't recognize it for another two years, this lecture marked the beginning of my work as a feminist critic of science. In it I raised three of the central questions that were to mark my research and writing over the next decade. I can now see that, with the concluding remarks of that lecture, I had also completed the basic shift in mind-set that made it possible to begin such a venture. Even though my views about gender, science, knowledge, and truth were to evolve considerably over the years to come, I had already made the two most essential steps: I had shifted attention from the question of male and female nature to that of *beliefs about* male and female nature, that is, to gender ideology. And I had admitted the possibility that such beliefs could affect science itself.

In hindsight, these two moves may seem simple enough, but when I reflect on my own history, as well as that of other women scientists, I can see that they were not. Indeed, from my earlier vantage point, they were unthinkable. In that mind-set, there was room neither for a distinction between sexual identity and beliefs about sexual identity (not even for the prior distinction between sex and gender upon which it depends), nor for the possibility that beliefs could affect science—a possibility that requires a distinction analogous to that between sex and gender, only now between nature and science. I was, of course, able to accommodate a distinction between belief and reality, but only in the sense of "false" beliefs—that is, mere illusion, or mere prejudice; "true" beliefs I took to be synonymous with the "real."

It seems to me that in that mind-set, beliefs per se were not seen as having any real force—neither the force to shape the development of men and women, nor the force to shape the development of science. Some people may "misperceive" nature, human or otherwise, but properly seen, men and women simply *are*, faithful reflections of male and female biology—just as science simply *is*, a faithful reflection of nature. Gravity has (or is) a force, DNA has force, but beliefs do not. In other words, as scientists, we are trained to see the locus of real force in the world as physical, not mental.

There is of course a sense in which they are right: Beliefs per se cannot exert force on the world. But the people who carry such beliefs can. Furthermore, the language in which their beliefs are encoded has the force to shape what others—as men, as women, and as scientists—think, believe, and, in turn, actually do. It may have taken the lens of feminist theory to reveal the popular association of science, objectivity, and masculinity as a statement about the social rather than natural (or biological) world, referring not to the bodily and mental capacities of individual men and women, but to a collective consciousness; that is, as a set of beliefs given existence by language rather than by bodies, and by that language, granted the force to shape what individual men and women might (or might not) do. But to see how such culturally laden language could contribute to the shaping of science takes a different kind of lens. That requires, first and foremost, a recognition of the social character (and force) of the enterprise we call "science," a recognition quite separable from—and in fact, historically independent of—the insights of contemporary feminism.

SHANNON BROWNLEE

CAN'T DO WITHOUT LOVE
What Science Says about
Those Tender Feelings

Love has toppled kings, inspired poets, sparked wars, soothed beasts, and changed the course of history. It is credited for life's greatest joys, blamed for the most crushing sorrows. And of course, it "makes the world go round."

All of which is no surprise to biologists. They know that love is central to human existence. We are not just programmed for reproduction: The capacity for loving emotions is also written into our biochemistry, essential if children are to grow and to thrive. And love's absence can be devastating: The loss of a spouse often hastens death in older people.

Now researchers are beginning to sort out how body and mind work together to produce the wild, tender, ineffable feelings we call love. They have found, for example, that oxytocin, a chemical that fosters the bond between mothers and children, probably helps fuel romantic love as well. Brain chemicals that blunt pain and induce feelings of euphoria may also make people feel good in the company of lovers. And certain other mammals share many of the same neural and chemical pathways involved in human love—though no one knows if they feel a similar swooning intensity of emotion.

Far from reducing love's thrill to dry facts, biologists' efforts underscore the emotion's importance. "We evolved as social organisms," says University of Maryland zoologist Sue Carter. "The study of love tells us that we have a biology that allows us to be good to each other."

MOTHER, MOTHER

Love began with motherhood. For mammalian young to survive, mothers must invest considerable time and energy in them. Of course, the varying growth rates of mammalian species require some mothers to invest more time and energy than others. An elephant seal suckles her pup for only a few weeks before abandoning it; other species, including elephants, some primates, and especially people, lavish attention on their young for years.

With the help of oxytocin, doting mothers are able to cater to their offspring's every whim and whimper. When females of most mammalian species give birth, their bodies are flooded with oxytocin, known since 1906 as a hormone that stimulates uterine contractions and allows the breasts to "let down" milk. But oxytocin also acts as a neurotransmitter, or chemical messenger, that can guide behavior. Without it, a ewe cannot recognize her own lamb. A virgin female rat given a shot of oxytocin will nuzzle another female's pups, crouching over them protectively as if they were her own.

Oxytocin has even more dramatic effects on human mothers, inducing a tender openness that fosters maternal devotion. As a mother breast-feeds, oxytocin levels rise in her blood. She also scores higher on psychological measures of "social desirability," the urge to please others, according to Kerstin Uvnas-Moberg of Sweden's Karolinska Institute. Mothers with higher levels of oxytocin are more sensitive to other people's feelings and better at reading nonverbal cues than those with lower levels. This makes sense, says Uvnas-Moberg, because oxytocin is thought to bind to centers in the brain involved with emotion. In her most recent experiments, the scientist has found that oxytocin acts as a natural tranquilizer, lowering a new mother's blood pressure, blunting her sensitivity to pain and stress, and perhaps helping her view her child more as a bundle of joy than as a burden.

Studies of a small rodent known as the prairie vole, a cuddly ball of fur whose mating bond of lifelong monogamy would put most human couples to shame, indicate oxytocin may also play a role in the heady feelings associated with romance. "You just can't imagine how much time these animals spend together. Prairie voles always want to be with somebody," says Carter. The voles' undying devotion is the work not only of oxytocin but also of a related hormone, vasopressin. When single male and female prairie voles meet, they commence a two-day-long bout of sex that releases oxytocin in the female's brain, bonding her to the male. Deprived of the chemical, she finds him no more appealing than any other vole. Given an injection of oxytocin, she will prefer the vole she's with, whether or not they have consummated their relationship. Vasopressin inspires similar ardor in the male, who prefers his mate's company above all others, guarding his family against intruders with a jealous husband's zeal.

Like some human playboys, male prairie voles seem to get a kick out of courtship mixed with danger. Carter and colleague Courtney DeVries made young, unmated voles swim for three minutes before allowing them to meet a prospective mate. The exercise elevated the animals' stress hormones, which are also heightened by fear. But while females scurried off after the swim without bonding to the males as they normally would, male voles bonded faster than ever.

LURE OF THE FORBIDDEN

Human beings—unlike rodents—are not entirely slaves to their hormones. But the behavior of voles may hold clues to why men and women sometimes hold divergent views of sex and romance. While many women prefer candlelight and sweet talk, men are more apt to welcome a roll in the hay anytime, anywhere. For some men (and some women), sex is especially enticing when forbidden. Carter and DeVries suspect stress hormones can interfere with oxytocin's action in the brain, keeping a female vole from bonding, and perhaps preventing most women from finding danger sexually exciting. Vasopressin, in contrast, appears to work better in the presence of certain stress hormones, possibly making danger an aphrodisiac for many males.

Love's other messengers in the brain are the endorphins, or brain opiates—the body's own version of drugs such as heroin and morphine. High levels of brain opiates kill pain and induce a state of happy relaxation. Low levels are associated with unpleasant feelings. Researchers believe the power of endorphins to affect mood may play a crucial role in bonding.

Compelling evidence for this notion comes from recent studies of female talapoin monkeys, animals that form what in humans would be termed friendships. While male talapoins are bellicose and standoffish, female talapoin friends spend as much as a third of their day grooming each other and twining their long tails together. Barry Keverne, a primatologist at Cambridge University in England, has found that when talapoin friends who have been separated are reunited, they commence grooming enthusiastically—and their endorphins skyrocket to double the usual level. Separated monkeys given a low dose of morphine, however, show little interest in grooming upon reunion: Since their opiate levels are already high, they don't need each other to feel good again. "It's not surprising that the same opioid system that evolved to modulate physical pain also can soothe the pain of social isolation," says Jaak Panksepp of Ohio's Bowling Green State University.

Indeed, research on opiates suggests the flip side of love is not hate, but grief. "Biochemically, loss of love, or grief, is the inverse of love," says Keverne. Nobody has yet proved that people get an endorphin kick out of love or friendship. But the human brain shares so much of its emotional chemistry with close evolutionary relatives, it's not unlikely that human lovers and friends enjoy a soothing surge of endorphins when they meet—and miss that feeling when separated.

Passionate or platonic, love affects the whole body, setting the heart pounding, making the stomach do flip-flops, and of course, lighting the loins on fire. These visceral sensations are the work of the vagus nerve, which traces a meandering path through the body, coordinating the activities of internal organs, says the University of Maryland's Stephen Porges. The vagus ferries signals between our innards and our brains, conveying information upward about our internal state and sending orders down from the brain to the heart, the stomach, the lungs, and the sex organs.

Without the vagus, says Porges, love would be impossible. One part of the nerve is evolutionarily ancient, controlling primitive functions such as sex, hunger, and fear. This "old" vagus responds to oxytocin and serves as the pathway between sexual organs and the brain for feelings of both arousal and satiation after sex. But Porges argues that in mammals, newer branches of the vagus also connect emotional brain centers with the heart, the face, and the vocal equipment, helping to coordinate feelings with facial and verbal expression. The "new" vagus also helps slow the heart and keep the body calm enough for the brain to pay attention to emotional signals from other people. Without this, says Porges, "we can't modulate our interiors enough to express or read emotions."

In other words, the poets and bards were right about one thing: The heart speaks the language of love. As English poet W. H. Auden wrote, Where love is strengthened, hope restored, / In hearts by chemical accord. It may not literally skip a beat at the sight of one's desire or break with sorrow, but the heart's rhythms are exquisitely tuned to love.

DEBORAH TANNEN

SEX, LIES, AND CONVERSATION

I was addressing a small gathering in a suburban Virginia living room—a women's group that had invited men to join them. Throughout the evening, one man had been particularly talkative, frequently offering ideas and anecdotes, while his wife sat silently beside him on the couch. Toward the end of the evening, I commented that women frequently complain that their husbands don't talk to them. This man quickly concurred. He gestured toward his wife and said, "She's the talker in our family." The room burst into laughter; the man looked puzzled and hurt. "It's true," he explained. "When I come home from work I have nothing to say. If she didn't keep the conversation going, we'd spend the whole evening in silence."

This episode crystallizes the irony that although American men tend to talk more than women in public situations, they often talk less at home. And this pattern is wreaking havoc with marriage.

The pattern was observed by political scientist Andrew Hacker in the late '70s. Sociologist Catherine Kohler Riessman reports in her new book *Divorce Talk* that most of the women she interviewed—but only a few of the men—gave lack of communication as the reason for their divorces. Given the current divorce rate of nearly 50 percent, that amounts to millions of cases in the United States every year—a virtual epidemic of failed conversation.

In my own research, complaints from women about their husbands most often focused not on tangible inequities such as having given up the chance for a career to accompany a husband to his, or doing far more than their share of daily life—support work like cleaning, cooking, social arrangements and errands. Instead, they focused on communication: "He doesn't listen to me," "He doesn't talk to me." I found, as Hacker observed years before, that most wives want their husbands to be, first and foremost, conversational partners, but few husbands share this expectation of their wives.

In short, the image that best represents the current crisis is the stereotypical cartoon scene of a man sitting at the breakfast table with a newspaper held up in front of his face while a woman glares at the back of it, wanting to talk.

LINGUISTIC BATTLE OF THE SEXES

How can women and men have such different impressions of communication in marriage? Why the widespread imbalance in their interests and expectations?

In the April issue of *American Psychologist*, Stanford University's Eleanor Macoby reports the results of her own and others' research showing their children's development is most influenced by the social structure of peer interactions. Boys and girls tend to play with children of their own gender, and their sex-separate groups have different organizational structures and interactive norms.

I believe these systematic differences in childhood socialization make talk between women and men like cross-cultural communication, heir to all the attraction and pitfalls of that enticing but difficult enterprise. My research on men's and women's conversations uncovered patterns similar to those described for children's groups.

For women, as for girls, intimacy is the fabric of relationships, and talk is the thread from which it is woven. Little girls create and maintain friendships by exchanging secrets; similarly, women regard conversation as the cornerstone of friendship. So a woman expects her husband to be a new and improved version of a best friend. What is important is not the individual subjects that are discussed but the sense of closeness of a life shared, that emerges when people tell their thoughts, feelings, and impressions.

Bonds between boys can be as intense as girls, but they are based less on talking, more on doing things together. Since they don't assume talk is the cement that binds a relationship men don't know what kind of talk women want, and they don't miss it when it isn't there.

Boys' groups are larger, more inclusive, and more hierarchical, so boys must struggle to avoid the subordinate position in the group. This may play a role in women's complaints that men don't listen to them. Some men really don't like to listen, because being the listener makes them feel one-down, like a child listening to adults or an employee to a boss.

But often when women tell men, "You aren't listening," and the men protest, "I am," the men are right. The impression of not listening results from misalignments in the mechanics of conversation. The misalignment begins as soon as a man and a woman take physical positions. This became clear when I studied videotapes made by psychologist Bruce Dorval of children and adults talking to their same-sex best friends. I found that at every age, the girls and women faced each other directly, their eyes anchored on each other's faces. At every age, the boys and men sat at angles to each other and looked elsewhere in the room, periodically glancing at each other. They were obviously attuned to each other, often mirroring each other's movements. But the tendency of men to face away can give women the impression they aren't listening even when they are. A young woman in college was frustrated: Whenever she told her boyfriend she wanted to talk to him, he would lie down on the floor, close his eyes, and put his arm over his face. This signaled to her "He's taking a nap." But he insisted he was listening extra-hard. Normally, he looks around the room, so he is easily distracted. Lying down and covering his eyes helped him concentrate on what she was saying.

Analogous to the physical alignment that women and men take in conversation is their topical alignment. The girls in my study tended to talk at length about one topic, but the boys tended to jump from topic to topic. The second-grade girls exchanged stories about people they knew. The second-grade boys teased, told jokes, noticed things in the room and talked about finding games to play. The sixth-grade girls talked about problems with a mutual friend. The sixth-grade boys talked about 55 different topics, none of which extended over more than a few turns.

LISTENING TO BODY LANGUAGE

Switching topics is another habit that gives women the impression men aren't listening, especially if they switch to a topic about themselves. But the evidence of the 10th-grade boys in my study indicates otherwise. The 10th-grade boys sprawled across their chairs with bodies parallel and eyes straight ahead, rarely looking at each other. They looked as if they were riding in a car, staring out the windshield. But they were talking about their feelings. One boy was upset because a girl had told him he had a drinking problem, and the other was feeling alienated from all his friends.

Now, when a girl told a friend about a problem, the friend responded by asking probing questions and expressing agreement and understanding. But the boys dismissed each other's problems. Todd assured Richard that his drinking was "no big problem" because "sometimes you're funny when you're off your butt." And when Todd said he felt left out, Richard responded, "Why should you? You know more people than me."

Women perceive such responses as belittling and unsupportive. But the boys seemed satisfied with them. Whereas women reassure each other by implying, "You shouldn't feel bad because I've had similar experiences," men do so by implying. "You shouldn't feel bad because your problems aren't so bad."

There are even simpler reasons for women's impression that men don't listen. Linguist Lynette Hirschman found that women make more listener-noise, such as "mhm," "uhuh," and "yeah," to show "I'm with you." Men, she found, more often give silent attention. Women who expect a stream of listener-noise interpret silent attention as no attention at all.

Women's conversational habits are as frustrating to men as men's are to women. Men who expect silent attention interpret a stream of listener-noise as overreaction or impatience. Also, when women talk to each other in a close, comfortable setting, they often overlap, finish each other's sentences and anticipate what the other is about to say. This practice, which I call "participatory listenership," is often perceived by men as interruption, intrusion and lack of attention.

A parallel difference caused a man to complain about his wife, "She just wants to talk about her own point of view. If I show her another view, she gets mad at me." When most women talk to each other, they assume a conversationalist's job is to express agreement and support. But many men see their conversational duty as pointing out the other side of an argument. This is heard as disloyalty by women, and refusal to offer the requisite support. It is not that women don't want to see other points of view, but that they prefer them phrased as suggestions and inquiries rather than as direct challenges.

In his book *Fighting for Life*, Walter Ong points out that men use "agonistic" or warlike, oppositional formats to do almost anything; thus discussion becomes debate, and conversation a competitive sport. In contrast, women see conversation as a ritual means of establishing rapport. If Jane tells a problem and June says she has a similar one, they walk away feeling closer to each other. But this attempt at establishing rapport can backfire when used with men. Men take too literally women's ritual "troubles talk," just as women mistake men's ritual challenges for real attack.

THE SOUNDS OF SILENCE

These differences begin to clarify why women and men have such different expectations about communication in marriage. For women, talk creates intimacy. Marriage is an orgy of closeness: you can tell your feelings and thoughts, and still be loved. Their greatest fear is being pushed away. But men live in a hierarchical world, where talk maintains independence and status. They are on guard to protect themselves from being put down and pushed around.

This explains the paradox of the talkative man who said of his silent wife, "She's the talker." In the public setting of a guest lecture, he felt challenged to show his intelligence and display his understanding of the lecture. But at home, where he has nothing to prove and no one to defend against, he is free to remain silent. For his wife, being home means she is free from the worry that something she says might offend someone, or spark disagreement, or appear to be showing off; at home she is free to talk.

The communication problems that endanger marriage can't be fixed by mechanical engineering. They require a new conceptual framework about the role of talk in human relationships. Many of the psychological explanations that have become second nature may not be helpful, because they tend to blame either women (for not being assertive enough) or men (for not being in touch with their feelings). A sociolinguistic approach by which male-female conversation is seen as cross-cultural communication allows us to understand the problem and forge solutions without blaming either party.

Once the problem is understood, improvement comes naturally, as it did to the young woman and her boyfriend who seemed to go to sleep when she wanted to talk. Previously, she had accused him of not listening, and he had refused to change his behavior, since that would be admitting fault. But then she learned about and explained to him the differences in women's and men's habitual ways of aligning themselves in conversation. The next time she told him she wanted to talk, he began, as usual, by lying down and covering his eyes. When the familiar negative reaction bubbled up, she reassured herself that he really was listening. But then he sat up and looked at her. Thrilled, she asked why. He said, "You like me to look at you when we talk, so I'll try to do it." Once he saw their differences as cross-cultural rather than right and wrong, he independently altered his behavior.

Women who feel abandoned and deprived when their husband won't listen to or report daily news may be happy to discover their husbands trying to adapt once they understand the place of small talk in women's relationships. But if their husbands don't adapt, the women may still be comforted that for men, this is not a failure of intimacy. Accepting the difference, the wives may look to their friends or family for that kind of talk. And husbands who can't provide it shouldn't feel their wives have made unreasonable demands. Some couples will still decide to divorce, but at least their decisions will be based on realistic expectations.

In these times of resurgent ethnic conflicts, the world desperately needs cross-cultural understanding. Like charity, successful cross-cultural communication should begin at home.

STEPHEN JAY GOULD

WORM FOR A CENTURY, AND ALL SEASONS

In the preface to his last book, an elderly Charles Darwin wrote: "The subject may appear an insignificant one, but we shall see that it possesses some interest; and the maxim 'de minimis lex non curat' [the law is not concerned with trifles] does not apply to science."

Trifles may matter in nature, but they are unconventional subjects for last books. Most eminent graybeards sum up their life's thought and offer a few pompous suggestions for reconstituting the future. Charles Darwin wrote about worms—*The Formation of Vegetable Mould, Through the Action of Worms, With Observations on Their Habits* (1881).

This month[1] marks the one-hundredth anniversary of Darwin's death— and celebrations are under way throughout the world. Most symposiums and books are taking the usual high road of broad implication—Darwin and modern life, or Darwin and evolutionary thought. For my personal tribute, I shall take an ostensibly minimalist stance and discuss Darwin's "worm book." But I do this to argue that Darwin justly reversed the venerable maxim of his legal colleagues.

1. Darwin died on April 19, 1882 and this column first appeared in *Natural History* in April 1982.

Darwin was a crafty man. He liked worms well enough, but his last book, although superficially about nothing else, is (in many ways) a covert summation of the principles of reasoning that he had labored a lifetime to identify and use in the greatest transformation of nature ever wrought by a single man. In analyzing his concern with worms, we may grasp the sources of Darwin's general success.

The book has usually been interpreted as a curiosity, a harmless work of little importance by a great naturalist in his dotage. Some authors have even used it to support a common myth about Darwin that recent scholarship has extinguished. Darwin, his detractors argued, was a man of mediocre ability who became famous by the good fortune of his situation in place and time. His revolution was "in the air" anyway, and Darwin simply had the patience and pertinacity to develop the evident implications. He was, Jacques Barzon once wrote (in perhaps the most inaccurate epitome I have ever read), "a great assembler of facts and a poor joiner of ideas . . . a man who does not belong with the great thinkers."

To argue that Darwin was merely a competent naturalist mired in trivial detail, these detractors pointed out that most of his books are about minutiae or funny little problems—the habits of climbing plants, why flowers of different form are sometimes found on the same plant, how orchids are fertilized by insects, four volumes on the taxonomy of barnacles, and finally, how worms churn the soil. Yet all these books have both a manifest and a deeper or implicit theme—and detractors missed the second (probably because they didn't read the books and drew conclusions from the titles alone). In each case, the deeper subject is evolution itself or a larger research program for analyzing history in a scientific way.

Why is it, we may ask at this centenary of his passing, that Darwin is still so central a figure in scientific thought? Why must we continue to read his books and grasp his vision if we are to be competent natural historians? Why do scientists, despite their notorious unconcern with history, continue to ponder and debate his works? Three arguments might be offered for Darwin's continuing relevance to scientists.

We might honor him first as the man who "discovered" evolution. Although popular opinion may grant Darwin this status, such an accolade is surely misplaced, for several illustrious predecessors shared his conviction that organisms are linked by ties of physical descent. In nineteenth-century biology, evolution was a common enough heresy.

As a second attempt, we might locate Darwin's primary claim upon continued scientific attention in the extraordinarily broad and radical implications of his proffered evolutionary mechanism—natural selection. Indeed, I have pushed this theme relentlessly in my two previous books, focusing upon three arguments: natural selection as a theory of local adaptation, not inexorable progress; the claim that order in nature arises as a coincidental by-product of struggle among individuals; and the materialistic character of Darwin's theory, particularly his denial of any causal role to spiritual forces, energies, or powers. I do not now abjure this theme, but I have come to realize that it cannot represent the major reason for Darwin's continued *scientific* relevance, though it does account for his impact upon the world at large. For it is too grandiose, and working scientists rarely traffic in such abstract generality.

Everyone appreciates a nifty idea or an abstraction that makes a person sit up, blink hard several times to clear the intellectual cobwebs, and reverse a cherished opinion. But science deals in the workable and soluble, the idea that can be fruitfully embodied in concrete objects suitable for poking, squeezing, manipulating, and extracting. The idea that counts in science must lead to fruitful work, not only to speculation that does not engender empirical test, no matter how much it stretches the mind.

I therefore wish to emphasize a third argument for Darwin's continued importance, and to claim that his greatest achievement lay in establishing principles of *useful* reason for sciences (like evolution) that attempt to reconstruct history. The special problems of historical science (as contrasted, for example, with experimental physics) are many, but one stands out most prominently: Science must identify processes that yield observed results. The results of history lie strewn around us, but we cannot, in principle, directly observe the processes that produced them. How then can we be scientific about the past?

As a general answer, we must develop criteria for inferring the processes we cannot see from results that have been preserved. This is the quintessential problem of evolutionary theory: How do we use the anatomy, physiology, behavior, variation, and geographic distribution of modern organisms, and the fossil remains in our geological record, to infer the pathways of history?

Thus, we come to the covert theme of Darwin's worm book, for it is both a treatise on the habits of earthworms and an exploration of how we can approach history in a scientific way.

Darwin's mentor, the great geologist Charles Lyell, had been obsessed with the same problem. He argued, though not with full justice, that his predecessors had failed to construct a science of geology because they had not developed procedures for inferring an unobservable past from a surrounding present and had therefore indulged in unprovable reverie and speculation. "We see," he wrote in his incomparable prose, "the ancient spirit of speculation revived and a desire manifestly shown to cut, rather than patiently to untie, the Gordian Knot." His solution, an aspect of the complex world view later called uniformitarianism, was to observe the work of present processes and to extrapolate their rates and effects into the past. Here Lyell faced a problem. Many results of the past—the Grand Canyon for example—are extensive and spectacular, but most of what goes on about us every day doesn't amount to much—a bit of erosion here or deposition there. Even a Stromboli or a Vesuvius will cause only local devastation. If modern forces do too little, then we must invoke more cataclysmic processes, now expired or dormant, to explain the past. And we are in catch-22: if past processes were effective and different from present processes, we might explain the past in principle, but we could not be scientific about it because we have no modern analogue in what we can observe. If we rely only upon present processes, we lack sufficient oomph to render the past.

Lyell sought salvation in the great theme of geology: time. He argued that the vast age of our earth provides ample time to render all observed results, however spectacular, by the simple summing of small changes over immense periods. Our failure lay, not with the earth, but with our habits of mind: we had been previously unwilling to recognize how much work the most insignificant processes can accomplish with enough time.

Darwin approached evolution in the same way. The present becomes relevant, and the past therefore becomes scientific, only if we can sum the small effects of present processes to produce observed results. Creationists did not use this principle and therefore failed to understand the relevance of small-scale variation that pervades the biological world (from breeds of dogs to geographical variation in butterflies). Minor variations are the stuff of evolution (not merely a set of accidental excursions around a created ideal type), but we recognize this only when we are prepared to sum small effects through long periods of time.

Darwin recognized that this principle, as a basic mode of reasoning in historical science, must extend beyond evolution. Thus, late in his life, he decided to abstract and exemplify his historical method by applying it to a problem apparently quite different from evolution—a project broad enough to cap an illustrious career. He chose earthworms and the soil. Darwin's refutation of the legal maxim "de minimis lex non curat" was a conscious double-entendre. Worms are both humble and interesting, and a worm's work, when summed over all worms and long periods of time, can shape our landscape and form our soils.

Thus, Darwin wrote at the close of his preface, refuting the opinions of a certain Mr. Fish who denied that worms could account for much "considering their weakness and their size":

> Here we have an instance of that inability to sum up the effects of a continually recurrent cause, which has often retarded the progress of science, as formerly in the case of geology, and more recently in that of the principle of evolution.

Darwin had chosen well to illustrate his generality. What better than worms: the most ordinary, commonplace, and humble objects of our daily observation and dismissal. If they, working constantly beneath our notice, can form much of our soil and shape our landscape, then what event of magnitude cannot arise from the summation of small effects. Darwin had not abandoned evolution for earthworms; rather, he was using worms to illustrate the general method that had validated evolution as well. Nature's mills, like God's, grind both slowly and exceedingly small.

Darwin made two major claims for worms. First, in shaping the land, their effects are directional. They triturate particles of rock into ever smaller fragments (in passing them through their gut while churning the soil), and they denude the land by loosening and disaggregating the soil as they churn it; gravity and erosive agents then move the soil more easily from high to low ground, thus leveling the landscape. The low, rolling character of topography in areas inhabited by worms is, in large part, a testimony to their slow but persistent work.

Second, in forming and churning the soil, they maintain a steady state amidst constant change. As the primary theme of his book (and the source of its title), Darwin set out to prove that worms form the soil's upper layer, the so-called vegetable mold. He describes it in the opening paragraph:

> The share which worms have taken in the formation of the layer of vegetable mould, which covers the whole surface of the land in every moderately humid country, is the subject of the present volume. This mould is generally of a blackish color and a few inches in thickness. In different districts it differs but little in appearance, although it may rest on various subsoils. The uniform fineness of the particles of which it is composed is one of its chief characteristic features.

Darwin argues that earthworms form vegetable mold by bringing "a large quantity of fine earth" to the surface and depositing it there in the form of castings. (Worms continually pass soil through their intestinal canals, extract anything they can use for food, and "cast" the rest; the rejected material is not feces but primarily soil particles, reduced in average size by trituration and with some organic matter removed.) The castings, originally spiral in form and composed of fine particles, are then disaggregated by wind and water, and spread out to form vegetable mold. "I was thus led to conclude," Darwin writes, "that all the vegetable mould over the whole country has passed many times through, and will again pass many times through, the intestinal canals of worms."

The mold doesn't continually thicken after its formation, for it is compacted by pressure into more solid layers a few inches below the surface. Darwin's theme here is not directional alteration, but continuous change within apparent constancy. Vegetable mold is always the same, yet always changing. Each particle cycles through the system, beginning at the surface in a casting, spreading out, and then working its way down as worms deposit new castings above; but the mold itself is not altered. It may retain the same thickness and character while all its particles cycle. Thus, a system that seems to us stable, perhaps even immutable, is maintained by constant turmoil. We who lack an appreciation of history and have so little feel for the aggregated importance of small but continuous change scarcely realize that the very ground is being swept from beneath our feet; it is alive and constantly churning.

Darwin uses two major types of arguments to convince us that worms form the vegetable mold. He first proves that worms are sufficiently numerous and widely spread in space and depth to do the job. He demonstrates "what a vast number of worms live unseen by us beneath our feet"— some 53,767 per acre (or 356 pounds of worms) in good British soil. He then gathers evidence from informants throughout the world to argue that worms are far more widely distributed, and in a greater range of apparently unfavorable environments, than we usually imagine. He digs to see how deeply they extend into the soil, and cuts one in two at fifty-five inches, although others report worms at eight feet down or more.

With plausibility established, he now seeks direct evidence for constant cycling of vegetable mold at the earth's surface. Considering both sides of the issue, he studies the foundering of objects into the soil as new castings pile up above them, and he collects and weighs the castings themselves to determine the rate of cycling.

Darwin was particularly impressed by the evenness and uniformity of foundering for objects that had once lain together at the surface. He sought fields that, twenty years or more before, had been strewn with objects of substantial size—burned coals, rubble from the demolition of a building, rocks collected from the plowing of a neighboring field. He trenched these fields and found, to his delight, that the objects still formed a clear layer, parallel to the surface but now several inches below it and covered with vegetable mold made entirely of fine particles. "The straightness and regularity of the lines formed by the embedded objects, and their parallelism with the surface of the land, are the most striking features of the case," he wrote. Nothing could beat worms for a slow and meticulous uniformity of action.

Darwin studied the sinking of "Druidical stones" at Stonehenge and the foundering of Roman bathhouses, but he found his most persuasive example at home, in his own field, last plowed in 1841:

> For several years it was clothed with an extremely scant vegetation, and was so thickly covered with small and large flints (some of them half as large as a child's head) that the field was always called by my sons "the stony field." When they ran down the slope the stones clattered together. I remember doubting whether I should live to see these larger flints covered with vegetable mould and turf. But the smaller stones disappeared before many years had elapsed, as did every one of the larger ones after a time; so that after thirty years (1871) a horse could gallop over the compact turf from one end of the field to the other and not strike a single stone with his shoes. To anyone who remembered the appearance of the field in 1842 the transformation was wonderful. This was certainly the work of the worms.

In 1871 he cut a trench in his field and found 2.5 inches of vegetable mold entirely free from flints: "Beneath this lay coarse clayey earth full of flints like that in any of the neighboring ploughed fields. . . . The average rate of accumulation of the mould during the whole thirty years was only .083 inch per year (i.e. nearly one inch in twelve years)."

In various attempts to collect and weigh castings directly, Darwin estimated from 7.6 to 18.1 tons per acre per year. Spread out evenly upon the surface he calculated that from 0.8 to 2.2 inches of mold would form anew every ten years. In gathering these figures Darwin relied upon that great unsung and so characteristically British institution—the corps of zealous amateurs in natural history, ready to endure any privation for a precious fact. I was particularly impressed by one anonymous contributor: "A lady" Darwin tells us "on whose accuracy I can implicitly rely, offered to collect during a year all the castings thrown up on two separate square yards, near Leith Hill Place, in Surrey." Was she the analogue of a modern Park

Avenue woman of means, carefully scraping up after her dog: one bag for a cleaner New York, the other for Science with a capital S?

The pleasure of reading Darwin's worm book lies not only in recognizing its larger point but also in the charm of detail that Darwin provides about worms themselves. I would rather peruse 300 pages of Darwin on worms than slog through 30 pages of eternal verities explicitly preached by many writers. The worm book is a labor of love and intimate, meticulous detail. In the book's other major section, Darwin spends 100 pages describing experiments to determine which ends of leaves (and triangular paper cutouts, or abstract "leaves") worms pull into their burrows first. Here we also find an overt and an underlying theme, in this case leaves and burrows versus the evolution of instinct and intelligence, Darwin's concern with establishing a usable definition of intelligence, and his discovery (under that definition) that intelligence pervades "lower" animals as well. All great science is a fruitful marriage of detail and generality, exultation and explanation. Both Darwin and his beloved worms left no stone unturned.

I have argued that Darwin's last book is a work on two levels—an explicit treatise on worms and the soil and a covert discussion of how to learn about the past by studying the present. But was Darwin consciously concerned with establishing a methodology for historical science, as I have argued, or did he merely stumble into such generality in his last book? I believe that his worm book follows the pattern of all his other works, from first to last: every compendium on minutiae is also a treatise on historical reasoning—and each book elucidates a different principle.

Consider his first book on a specific subject, *The Structure and Distribution of Coral-Reefs* (1842). In it, he proposed a theory for the formation of atolls, "those singular rings of coral-land which rise abruptly out of the unfathomable ocean," that won universal acceptance after a century of subsequent debate. He argued that coral reefs should be classified into three categories—fringing reefs that abut an island or continent, barrier reefs separated from island or continent by a lagoon, and atolls, or rings of reefs, with no platform in sight. He linked all three categories with his "subsidence theory," rendering them as three stages of a single process: the subsidence of an island or continental platform beneath the waves as living coral continues to grow upward. Initially, reefs grow right next to the platform (fringing reefs). As the platform sinks, reefs grow up and outward, leaving a separation between sinking platform and living coral (a barrier reef). Finally the platform sinks entirely, and a ring of coral expresses its former shape (an atoll). Darwin found the forms of modern reefs "inexplicable, excepting on the theory that their rocky bases slowly and successively sank beneath the level of the sea, whilst the corals continued to grow upwards."

This book is about coral, but it is also about historical reasoning. Vegetable mold formed fast enough to measure its rate directly; we capture the past by summing effects of small and observable present causes. But what if rates are too slow, or scales too large, to render history by direct observation of present processes? For such cases, we must develop a different method. Since large-scale processes begin at different times and proceed at diverse rates, the varied stages of different examples should exist simultaneously in the present. To establish history in such cases, we must construct a theory that will explain a series of present phenomena as stages of a single historical process. The method is quite general. Darwin used it to explain the formation of coral reefs. We invoke it today to infer the history of stars. Darwin also employed it to establish organic evolution itself. Some species are just beginning to split from their ancestors, others are midway through the process, still others are on the verge of completing it.

But what if evidence is limited to the static object itself? What if we can neither watch part of its formation nor find several stages of the process that produced it? How can we infer history from a lion? Darwin treated this problem in his treatise on the fertilization of orchids by insects (1862); the book that directly followed the *Origin of Species*. I have discussed his solution in several essays (1, 4, 11 and *The Panda's Thumb*) and will not dwell on it here: we infer history from imperfections that record constraints of descent. The "various contrivances" that orchids use to attract insects and attach pollen to them are the highly altered parts of ordinary flowers, evolved in ancestors for other purposes. Orchids work well enough, but they are jury-rigged to succeed because flowers are not optimally constructed for modification to these altered roles. If God wanted to make insect attractors and pollen stickers from scratch, he would certainly have built differently.

Thus, we have three principles for increasing adequacy of data: if you must work with a single object, look for imperfections that record historical descent; if several objects are available, try to render them as stages of a single historical process; if processes can be directly observed, sum up their effects through time. One may discuss these principles directly or recognize the "little problems" that Darwin used to exemplify them: orchids, coral reefs, and worms—the middle book, the first, and the last.

Darwin was not a conscious philosopher. He did not, like Huxley and Lyell, write explicit treatises on methodology. Yet I do not think he was unaware of what he was doing, as he cleverly composed a series of books at two levels, thus expressing his love for nature in the small and his ardent desire to establish both evolution and the principles of historical science. I was musing on this issue as I completed the worm book two weeks ago. Was Darwin really conscious of what he had done as he wrote his last professional lines, or did he proceed intuitively, as men of his genius sometimes do? Then I came to the very last paragraph, and I shook with the joy of insight. Clever old man; he knew full well. In his last words, he looked back to his beginning, compared those worms with his first corals, and completed his life's work in both the large and the small:

> The plough is one of the most ancient and most valuable of man's inventions; but long before he existed the land was in fact regularly ploughed, and still continues to be thus ploughed by earthworms. It may be doubted whether there are many other animals which have played so important a part in the history of the world, as have these lowly organized creatures. Some other animals, however, still more lowly organized, namely corals, have done more conspicuous work in having constructed innumerable reefs and islands in the great oceans; but these are almost confined to the tropical zones.

At the risk of unwarranted ghoulishness, I cannot suppress a final irony. A year after publishing his worm book, Darwin died on April 19, 1882. He wished to be buried in the soil of his adopted village, where he would have made a final and corporeal gift to his beloved worms. But the sentiments (and politicking) of fellow scientists and men of learning secured a guarded place for his body within the well-mortared floor of Westminster Abbey. Ultimately the worms will not be cheated, for there is no permanence in history, even for cathedrals. But ideas and methods have all the immortality of reason itself. Darwin has been gone for a century, yet he is with us whenever we choose to think about time.

JANE VAN LAWICK-GOODALL

FIRST OBSERVATIONS

For about a month I spent most of each day either on the Peak or over-looking Mlinda Valley where the chimps, before or after stuffing themselves with figs, ate large quantities of small purple fruits that tasted, like so many of their foods, as bitter and astringent as sloes or crab apples. Piece by piece, I began to form my first somewhat crude picture of chimpanzee life.

The impression that I had gained when I watched the chimps at the msulula tree of temporary, constantly changing associations of individuals within the community was substantiated. Most often I saw small groups of four to eight moving about together. Sometimes I saw one or two chimpanzees leave such a group and wander off on their own or join up with a different association. On other occasions I watched two or three small groups joining to form a larger one.

Often, as one group crossed the grassy ridge separating the Kasekela Valley from the fig trees on the home valley, the male chimpanzee, or chimpanzees of the party would break into a run, sometimes moving in an upright position, sometimes dragging a fallen branch, sometimes stamping or slapping the hard earth. These charging displays were always accompanied by loud pant-hoots and afterward the chimpanzee frequently would swing up into a tree overlooking the valley he was about to enter and sit quietly, peering down and obviously listening for a response from below. If there were chimps feeding in the fig trees they nearly always hooted back, as though in answer. Then the new arrivals would hurry down the steep slope and, with more calling and screaming, the two groups would meet in the fig trees. When groups of females and youngsters with no males present joined other feeding chimpanzees, usually there was none of this excitement; the newcomers merely climbed up into the trees, greeted some of those already there, and began to stuff themselves with figs.

While many details of their social behavior were hidden from me by the foliage, I did get occasional fascinating glimpses. I saw one female, newly arrived in a group, hurry up to a big male and hold her hand toward him. Almost regally he reached out, clasped her hand in his, drew it toward him, and kissed it with his lips. I saw two adult males embrace each other in greeting. I saw youngsters having wild games through the treetops, chasing around after each other or jumping again and again, one after the other, from a branch to a springy bough below. I watched small infants dangling happily by themselves for minutes on end, patting at their toes with one hand, rotating gently from side to side. Once two tiny infants pulled on opposite ends of a twig in a gentle tug-of-war. Often, during the heat of midday or after a long spell of feeding, I saw two or more adults grooming each other carefully looking through the hair of their companions.

At that time of year the chimps usually went to bed late, making their nests when it was too dark to see properly through binoculars, but sometimes they nested earlier and I could watch them from the Peak. I found that every individual, except for infants who slept with their mothers, made his own nest each night. Generally this took about three minutes: the chimp chose a firm foundation such as an upright fork or crotch, or two horizontal branches. Then he reached out and bent over smaller branches onto this foundation, keeping each one in place with his feet. Finally he tucked in the small leafy twigs growing around the rim of his nest and lay down. Quite often a chimp sat up after a few minutes and picked a handful of leafy twigs, which he put under his head or some other part of his body before settling down again for the night. One young female I watched went on and on bending down branches until she had constructed a huge mound of greenery on which she finally curled up.

I climbed up into some of the nests after the chimpanzees had left them. Most of them were built in trees that for me were almost impossible to climb. I found that there was quite complicated interweaving of the branches in some of them. I found, too, that the nests were not fouled with dung; and later, when I was able to get closer to the chimps, I saw how they were always careful to defecate and urinate over the edge of their nests, even in the middle of the night.

During that month I really came to know the country well, for I often went on expeditions from the Peak, sometimes to examine nests, more frequently to collect specimens of the chimpanzees' food plants, which Bernard Verdcourt had kindly offered to identify for me. Soon I could find my way around the sheer ravines and up and down the steep slopes of three valleys—the home valley, the Pocket, and Mlinda Valley—as well as a taxi driver finds his way about in the main streets and byways of London. It is a period I remember vividly, not only because I was beginning to accomplish something at last, but also because of the delight I felt in being completely by myself. For those who love to be alone with nature I need add nothing further; for those who do not, no words of mine could ever convey, even in part, the almost mystical awareness of beauty and eternity that accompanies certain treasured moments. And, though the beauty was always there, those moments came upon me unaware: when I was watching the pale flush preceding dawn; or looking up through the rustling leaves of some giant forest tree into the greens and browns and black shadows that occasionally ensnared a bright fleck of the blue sky; or when I stood, as darkness fell, with one hand on the still-warm trunk of a tree and looked at the sparkling of an early moon on the never still, sighing water of the lake.

One day, when I was sitting by the trickle of water in Buffalo Wood, pausing for a moment in the coolness before returning from a scramble in Mlinda Valley, I saw a female bushbuck moving slowly along the nearly dry streambed. Occasionally she paused to pick off some plant and crunch it. I kept absolutely still, and she was not aware of my presence until she was little more than ten yards away. Suddenly she tensed and stood staring at me, one small forefoot raised. Because I did not move, she did not know what I was—only that my outline was somehow strange. I saw her velvet nostrils dilate as she sniffed the air, but I was downwind and her nose gave her no answer. Slowly she came closer, and closer—one step at a time, her neck craned forward—always poised for instant flight. I can still scarcely believe that her nose actually touched my knee; yet if I close my eyes I can feel again, in imagination, the warmth of her breath and the silken impact of her skin. Unexpectedly I blinked and she was gone in a flash, bounding away with loud barks of alarm until the vegetation hid her completely from my view.

It was rather different when, as I was sitting on the Peak, I saw a leopard coming toward me, his tail held up straight. He was at a slightly lower level than I, and obviously had no idea I was there. Ever since arrival in Africa I had had an ingrained, illogical fear of leopards. Already, while working at the Gombe, I had several times nearly turned back when, crawling through some thick undergrowth, I had suddenly smelled the rank smell of cat. I had forced myself on, telling myself that my fear was foolish, that only wounded leopards charged humans with savage ferocity.

On this occasion, though, the leopard went out of sight as it started to climb up the hill—the hill on the peak of which I sat. I quickly hastened to climb a tree, but halfway there I realized that leopards can climb trees. So I uttered a sort of halfhearted squawk. The leopard, my logical mind told me, would be just as frightened of me if he knew I was there. Sure enough, there was a thudding of startled feet and then silence. I returned to the Peak, but the feeling of unseen eyes watching me was too much. I decided to watch for the chimps in Mlinda Valley. And, when I returned to the Peak several hours later, there, on the very rock which had been my seat, was a neat pile of leopard dung. He must have watched me go and then, very carefully, examined the place where such a frightening creature had been and tried to exterminate my alien scent with his own.

As the weeks went by the chimpanzees became less and less afraid. Quite often when I was on one of my food-collecting expeditions I came across chimpanzees unexpectedly, and after a time I found that some of them would tolerate my presence provided they were in fairly thick forest and I sat still and did not try to move closer than sixty to eighty yards. And so, during my second month of watching from the Peak, when I saw a group settle down to feed I sometimes moved closer and was thus able to make more detailed observations.

It was at this time that I began to recognize a number of different individuals. As soon as I was sure of knowing a chimpanzee if I saw it again, I named it. Some scientists feel that animals should be labeled by numbers—that to name them is anthropomorphic—but I have always been interested in the *differences* between individuals, and a name is not only more individual than a number but also far easier to remember. Most names were simply those which, for some reason or other, seemed to suit the individuals to whom I attached them. A few chimps were named because some facial expression or mannerism reminded me of human acquaintances.

The easiest individual to recognize was old Mr. McGregor. The crown of his head, his neck, and his shoulders were almost entirely devoid of hair, but a slight frill remained around his head rather like a monk's tonsure. He was an old male—perhaps between thirty and forty years of age (the longevity record of a captive chimp is forty-seven years). During the early months of my acquaintance with him, Mr. McGregor was somewhat belligerent. If I accidentally came across him at close quarters he would threaten me with an upward and backward jerk of his head and a shaking of branches before climbing down and vanishing from my sight. He reminded me, for some reason, of Beatrix Potter's old gardener in *The Tale of Peter Rabbit*.

Ancient Flo with her deformed, bulbous nose and ragged ears was equally easy to recognize. Her youngest offspring at that time were two-year-old Fifi, who still rode everywhere on her mother's back, and her juvenile son, Figan, who was always to be seen wandering around with his mother and little sister. He was then about six years old; it was approximately a year before he would attain puberty. Flo often traveled with another old mother, Olly. Olly's long face was also distinctive; the fluff of hair on the back of her head—though no other feature—reminded me of my aunt, Olwen. Olly, like Flo, was accompanied by two children, a daughter younger than Fifi, and an adolescent son about a year older than Figan.

Then there was William, who, I am certain, must have been Olly's blood brother. I never saw any special signs of friendship between them, but their faces were amazingly alike. They both had long upper lips that wobbled when they suddenly turned their heads. William had the added distinction of several thin, deeply etched scar marks running down his upper lip from his nose.

Two of the other chimpanzees I knew well by sight at that time were David Graybeard and Goliath. Like David and Goliath in the Bible, these two individuals were closely associated in my mind because they were very often together. Goliath, even in those days of his prime, was not a giant, but he had a splendid physique and the springy movements of an athlete. He probably weighed about one hundred pounds. David Graybeard was less afraid of me from the start than were any of the other chimps. I was always pleased when I picked out his handsome face and well-marked silvery beard in a chimpanzee group, for with David to calm the others, I had a better chance of approaching to observe them more closely.

Before the end of my trial period in the field I made two really exciting discoveries—discoveries that made the previous months of frustration well worth while. And for both of them I had David Graybeard to thank.

One day I arrived on the Peak and found a small group of chimps just below me in the upper branches of a thick tree. As I watched I saw that one of them was holding a pink-looking object from which he was from time to time pulling pieces with his teeth. There was a female and a youngster and they were both reaching out toward the male, their hands actually touching his mouth. Presently the female picked up a piece of the pink thing and put it to her mouth: it was at this moment that I realized the chimps were eating meat.

After each bite of meat the male picked off some leaves with his lips and chewed them with the flesh. Often, when he had chewed for several minutes on this leafy wad, he spat out the remains into the waiting hands of the female. Suddenly he dropped a small piece of meat, and like a flash the youngster swung after it to the ground. Even as he reached to pick it up the undergrowth exploded and an adult bushpig charged toward him. Screaming, the juvenile leaped back into the tree. The pig remained in the open, snorting and moving backward and forward. Soon I made out the shapes of three small striped piglets. Obviously the chimps were eating a baby pig. The size was right and later, when I realized that the male was David Graybeard, I moved closer and saw that he was indeed eating piglet.

For three hours I watched the chimps feeding. David occasionally let the female bite pieces from the carcass and once he actually detached a small piece of flesh and placed it in her outstretched hand. When he finally climbed down there was still meat left on the carcass; he carried it away in one hand, followed by the others.

Of course I was not sure, then, that David Graybeard had caught the pig for himself, but even so, it was tremendously exciting to know that these chimpanzees actually ate meat. Previously scientists had believed that although these apes might occasionally supplement their diet with a few insects or small rodents and the like they were primarily vegetarians and fruit eaters. No one had suspected that they might hunt larger mammals.

It was within two weeks of this observation that I saw something that excited me even more. By then it was October and the short rains had begun. The blackened slopes were softened by feathery new grass shoots and in some places the ground was carpeted by a variety of flowers. The Chimpanzees' Spring, I called it. I had had a frustrating morning, tramping up and down three valleys with never a sign or sound of a chimpanzee. Hauling myself up the steep slope of Mlinda Valley I headed for the Peak, not only weary but soaking wet from crawling through dense undergrowth. Suddenly I stopped, for I saw a slight movement in the long grass about sixty yards away. Quickly focusing my binoculars I saw that it was a single chimpanzee, and just then he turned in my direction. I recognized David Graybeard.

Cautiously I moved around so that I could see what he was doing. He was squatting beside the red earth mound of a termite nest, and as I watched I saw him carefully push a long grass stem down into a hole in the mound. After a moment he withdrew it and picked something from the end with his mouth. I was too far away to make out what he was eating, but it was obvious that he was actually using a grass stem as a tool.

I knew that on two occasions casual observers in West Africa had seen chimpanzees using objects as tools: one had broken open palm-nut kernels by using a rock as a hammer, and a group of chimps had been observed pushing sticks into an underground bees' nest and licking off the honey. Somehow I had never dreamed of seeing anything so exciting myself.

For an hour David feasted at the termite mound and then he wandered slowly away. When I was sure he had gone I went over to examine the mound. I found a few crushed insects strewn about, and a swarm of worker termites sealing the entrances of the nest passages into which David had obviously been poking his stems. I picked up one of his discarded tools and carefully pushed it into a hole myself. Immediately I felt the pull of several termites as they seized the grass, and when I pulled it out there were a number of worker termites and a few soldiers, with big red heads, clinging on with their mandibles. There they remained, sticking out at right angles to the stem with their legs waving in the air.

Before I left I trampled down some of the tall dry grass and constructed a rough hide—just a few palm fonds leaned up against the low branch of a tree and tied together at the top. I planned to wait there the next day. But it was another week before I was able to watch a chimpanzee "fishing" for termites again. Twice chimps arrived, but each time they saw me and moved off immediately. Once a swarm of fertile winged termites—the princes and princesses, as they are called—flew off on their nuptial flight, their huge white wings fluttering frantically as they carried the insects higher and higher. Later I realized that it is at this time of year, during the short rains, when the worker termites extend the passages of the nest to the surface, preparing for these emigrations. Several such swarms emerge between October and January. It is principally during these months that the chimpanzees feed on termites.

On the eighth day of my watch David Graybeard arrived again, together with Goliath, and the pair worked there for two hours. I could see much better: I observed how they scratched open the sealed-over passage entrances with a thumb or forefinger. I watched how they bit the end off their tools when they became bent, or used the other end, or discarded them in favor of new ones. Goliath once moved at least fifteen yards from the heap to select a firm-looking piece of vine, and both males often picked three or four stems while they were collecting tools, and put the spares beside them on the ground until they wanted them.

Most exciting of all, on several occasions they picked small leafy twigs and prepared them for use by stripping off the leaves. This was the first recorded example of a wild animal not merely using an object as a tool, but actually modifying an object and thus showing the crude beginnings of toolmaking.

Previously man had been regarded as the only tool-making animal. Indeed, one of the clauses commonly accepted in the definition of man was that he was a creature who "made tools to a regular and set pattern." The chimpanzees, obviously, had not made tools to any set pattern. Nevertheless, my early observations of their primitive toolmaking abilities convinced a number of scientists that it was necessary to redefine man in a more complex manner than before. Or else, as Louis Leakey put it, we should by definition have to accept the chimpanzee as Man.

HAUNANI KAY-TRASK

WOMEN'S "MANA" AND HAWAIIAN SOVEREIGNTY

*A*t the time I wrote this piece, the subject of Hawaiian women's leadership *was very much in the air in our movement. The men, in particular, were feeling unsupported and eclipsed by women's leadership. It is amazing to me that so many men feel personally injured when women take the lead, as if the only impact of our leadership is men's feelings.*

Lke our Maori siblings who struggle for sovereignty in the far reaches of the vast South Pacific, we Hawaiians in the isolated North Pacific have been working for the past twenty years to assert our genealogical claims as the indigenous people of Hawai'i. But unlike our Maori *'ohana*, we are not fighting within an independent island nation. Nor are we blessed with a large country where one island is sparsely populated. Nor are we fortunate enough to have but one major settler population with which to do battle.

No, we Hawaiians are, in many respects, among the most subordinated Natives in the Pacific Islands. Our land base is 1/16th the size of Aotearoa (New Zealand), and we are but one among five major ethnic groups in Hawai'i, two of which—the Japanese and the *haole*—are more populous and more economically powerful than Hawaiians. Our lands and waters have been inundated by foreigners, including the American military, and every kind of tourist.

The suffering and dispossession Hawaiians have endured—and continue to endure—have been justified by a racist ideology that claims we are better off as American citizens than we ever were as citizens of our own independent nation of Hawai'i. Despite the historical fact that Hawaiians did not want to become American citizens, and protested to this effect at the time of the overthrow in 1898, and again at annexation in 1898, our citizenship status has, according to American patriots, placed us in a select class of human beings. Allegedly, inclusion in the U.S. gave us "rights," the much-prized individual rewards that Americans wave in the faces of their conquered peoples, like little American flags on the graves of fallen soldiers. Universal suffrage, private property, and public education are among these "rights," as are the trumpeted joys of mass consumption, mass communication, and mass popular culture. Americans truly believe that such "rights" are the measure of civilization world-wide. Indeed, according to American ideology, every human being—whether from Africa, India, and the former Soviet Union, or the Americas, the Pacific Islands, and Asia—wants desperately to follow the American path by achieving such "rights." That these alleged "rights" were forced onto resisting peoples at the point of cannon and in the face of conquering armies is ignored in the case of Natives, like my own people, because the ideology of "rights" cannot abide the reality of imperialism.

By "rights" Americans do not mean Natives controlling their own affairs, holding their land and resources collectively as a people rather than as individuals, or learning and transmitting their own Native language, religion, and family structure.

Ideologically, "rights" talk is part of the larger, greatly obscured historical reality of American colonialism. The post-war American imperium is now global, as is the American denial that such an imperium exists. Part of this denial is the insistence that the United States has no colonies, only little island "democracies," like Puerto Rico, Micronesia, and Hawai'i. In these far-flung colonies, the language of "civil rights" operates to legitimize American control.

For example, by entering legalistic discussions wholly internal to the American system, Natives participate in their own mental colonization.

Once indigenous peoples begin to use terms like language "rights" and burial "rights," they are moving away from their cultural universe, from the understanding that language and burial places come out of our ancestral association with our lands of origin. These indigenous, Native practices are not "rights" which are given as the largesse of colonial governments. These practices are, instead, part of who we are, where we live, and how we feel.

When Hawaiians begin to think otherwise, that is, to think in terms of "rights," the identification as "Americans" is not far off. Thus, soon after annexation some of our people argued and organized for statehood, including members of my own family, because they believed control over their destiny as Hawaiians would be gained with full American citizenship such as the "right" to vote for the governor of the state of Hawai'i. Decades of work went into the statehood effort which was finally achieved in 1959.

Now, some 30 years later, Hawai'i is less Hawaiian, culturally, ecologically, and politically. Hawaiians themselves are fast outmigrating to California and other parts of the U.S. continent, and our islands have become the premier military fortress from which the U.S. patrols and nuclearizes the Pacific. Full American citizenship, i.e., full American "rights," thus accelerated the de-Hawaiianization begun with the theft of our government, lands, and language in the 1890's.

For us nationalist Hawaiians, the lesson of statehood is a lesson of loss and despair: the loss of land, of self-government, of language; the despair of political powerlessness, of cultural prostitution, of economic exploitation.

The franchise has given Hawaiians no control over our homelands (nearly 1.5 million acres including water and subsurface minerals), since they are held in alleged "trust" by the State and Federal governments, including the military. The right to a public education has not led to the creation of an educational system in the Hawaiian language, but rather to an education in a foreign language. And legal, i.e., judicial access has not been extended to Hawaiians as a people, despite a recent political battle of over five years' duration to wrest such access from the State. Still, in 1993, we have no standing in the courts to bring suit for breach of trust against our trustees, the State and Federal governments. Worse, the State is attempting to terminate their trust responsibilities by a one-time cash pay-off for all our lands. Now, post-statehood Hawai'i is a tinsel paradise for six-and-a-half million tourists a year, and a living nightmare for our impoverished, marginalized Native people.

While surviving as a Native person in any colonial situation is a strange mix of refusal and struggle with creation and assertion, the Hawaiian situation is particularly galling since the ideology of American democracy has both suppressed and co-opted Native resistance. Thus, when Hawaiians do begin to resist, we must start at the most elementary levels, such as challenging the preferability of Western dress, or the superiority of the English language. Slowly, this kind of challenge can proceed to larger, more political resistance, such as anti-military activity, efforts to preserve wetlands, forests, and other wild areas, and finally, a political struggle for self-determination.

The first stage of resistance involves a throwing off, or a peeling apart of a forced way of behaving. Layers of engineered assimilation begin to come loose in the face of alternatives, *Native cultural alternatives*. Usually, this process means tremendous psychological tension as a conscious rejection begins with cultural habits first ingrained by a colonial education, a foreign language, and a fearful daily relationship with the dominant, white class. Frantz Fanon identified this process as the birth of a new, revolutionary human being. Others, like the African writer Ngugi Wa Thiongo, call it "decolonizing the mind."

All across the Pacific Islands, and for at least the past forty years, Natives have been decolonizing their minds. Hawaiians, too, are participating in this same de-colonizing process, often mistakenly referred to as "cultural revival." Anthropologists and politicians readily use this term because it has no political context: the primary emphasis is usually on trivializing quaint practices and beliefs rather than on supporting conscious Native resistance to cultural imperialism. But decolonization is political at the core because it functions to unscrew the power of the colonizing force by creating a new consciousness very critical of foreign terms, foreign definitions, and foreign solutions.

Predictably, dangers arise in the early stages of decolonization, just as they do in any radicalizing process. For example, participation in Native culture merely as recreational activity stunts the growth of a critical political posture. By definition, recreational culture is peripheral—on the fringes rather than at the center of daily life. As recreation, this kind of cultural participation does not pose a direct, political challenge to the dominant forces within society, i.e., the very forces which control daily life. Worse, Hawaiian culture is constantly in danger of commercialization. Despite their real expression of our culture, the *hula* and Hawaiian language are easily incorporated into, and transformed by, tourist promotions, hotel festivities, and the ideological sea of commercialism that washes over our islands.

But paradoxically, recreational culture does create a rich medium for politicization. Even with the slick predations of tourism, things Hawaiian allow a re-enactment of cultural ways tied to our land, and our unique genealogical understanding of life. To counter the impulse toward commercialism, a politicizing agent must enter this medium, precipitating the growth of political consciousness. Sometimes, the agent is an elder whose cultural wisdom includes a sense of politics; at other times, the agent is an older friend or relative, what we call *kua'ana*, who consciously organizes and leads younger Hawaiians toward decolonization. These people operate in an already highly-politicized world where the push for sovereignty has been in the air for over ten years now. Their function is thus greatly aided by a common public understanding that sovereignty is a familiar demand and, given global resistance by colonial powers, a much-contested demand.

From my intimate participation in the Hawaiian movement for self-determination, it is obvious to me that these politicizing agents have most often been women—young, nationalist women. Occasionally, older women with cultural knowledge have evolved into nationalists, but they lead by virtue of their cultural *mana*, or power, rather than by political *mana*.

MANA

Now *mana*, in its Hawaiian sense, conveys an understanding that power is more than what the *haole* call charisma, or personal attraction. Leaders possess *mana*, they embody and display it. But the source of *mana* is not reducible to personal ability or spiritual and genealogical ancestry. A high chiefly line may bequeath the potential for *mana*, but the actualization or achievement of *mana* in terms of political leadership requires more than genealogy, it requires specific identification by the leader with the people, just as the *ali'i* or chiefs in days of old were judged by how well they cared for their people.

The presence of a leader with *mana* presupposes that the people acknowledge *mana* as an attribute of political leadership. Part of the beauty of Hawaiian decolonization is the re-assertion of *mana* in the sovereignty movement as a defining element of cultural and political leadership. Both the people and their leaders understand the link between *mana* and *pono*, the traditional Hawaiian value of balance between people, land, and the cosmos. Only a leader who understands this familial, genealogical link between Hawaiians and their land can hope to re-establish *pono*, the balance that has been lacking in the Hawaiian universe since the coming of the *haole*. The assertion of the value of *pono*, then, awaits a leader with *mana*.

In this decolonizing context, *mana,* as an attribute of leadership, is at once a tremendous challenge to the colonial system which defines political leadership in terms of democratic liberalism, that is, in terms of electoral victory, as well as a tremendous challenge to aspiring Hawaiian leaders who want to achieve sovereignty. By definition and history, leaders embody sovereignty only if they are *pono*, that is, only if they believe in and work for the wellbeing of the land and the people. In this way, Hawaiian leaders exhibit *mana* and increase it if they speak and represent the needs of Hawaiians, not the needs of all citizens of Hawai'i, or of legislative districts, or of bureaucratic institutions. *Mana*, then, opposes the American system of electoral power while reclaiming a form of political leadership based on Hawaiian cultural beliefs.

Hawaiian politicians who have chosen to subsume Hawaiian well-being under the need for profit, or as a peripheral concern to the larger concerns of all the people of Hawai'i *cannot* be *pono* leaders, nor can they be said to possess *mana*. Therefore, while the present governor of Hawai'i, John Waihe'e, is Hawaiian in ancestry, he does not behave as a Hawaiian leader should; that is, he does not work for the well-being of his people. For example, Waihe'e has submitted to the legislature a plan to extinguish all Hawaiian claims to our trust lands in exchange for money. On this point alone, Waihe'e has demonstrated that he is not a Hawaiian leader. Instead, Waihe'e is the leader of the Democratic Party, a typically American political machine whose sole purpose is to capture and maintain political office.

WOMEN'S MANA

Waihe'e is not alone as a Hawaiian politician; there are many others, including some female politicians, who have followed the male model of electoral politics. Indeed, a sizeable number of Hawaiians have chosen to assimilate into the foreign American system, including the first Hawaiian Senator in the U.S. Congress, Daniel Akaka. But while Hawaiian men have been transforming themselves into politicians, many Hawaiian women have chosen the path of decolonization, testing their leadership in the movement for sovereignty.

Because American culture, like Western civilization generally, is patriarchal, that is, structured and justified by values that emphasize male dominance over women and nature, American institutions reward men and male dominant behaviors with positions of power. This is how the patriarchy entrenches itself. Thus, the common reference to the public world, the world of politics and economics and bureaucracy as a "man's world" with the concomitant reference to the world of the family and of relationships as a "woman's world." Men are bred for power, women for powerlessness, except within their own sphere of the family.

Colonialism brought the replacement of the Hawaiian world by the *haole* world. Hawaiian women lost their place just as Hawaiian men lost theirs. Like most indigenous peoples colonized the world over, our marginalization meant economic ghettoization. We were to become a semi-skilled labor force for the *haole* capitalists. Above all, the loss of our land base denied us political and economic power.

During the long, 60-year darkness of the Territorial period, when immigrant Asian labor continued to outnumber our Native people while the *haole* tried desperately to retain their dominant position, some of our Hawaiian men slowly entered the legislature, organizing with Asian immigrant descendants for statehood and what they saw as their eventual takeover of political power. At statehood, some of our Native men, including my father and uncles, continued the transition into electoral power. They had been schooled in the American system and believed the only path to power lay through that system. Hawaiian ways, they reasoned, were gone forever; therefore, if Hawaiians were to improve their lot, they had to learn American ways. Of course, this is what Americanization seeks to do, namely, to convince conquered peoples they have no choice but to be Americanized. The ideology tells a tale of success: if one captures political power through the electoral process, one can do anything.

Anything, that is, except live as a Native person.

As our men sought power in the Americanized political system, they internalized the values of that system: politics is a man's world, family life is a woman's world. While some of our men, the most educated and articulate, rose up in the ranks of the political system, our women tended the home. Americanization had triumphed, at least on the surface.

But every generation surprises the one that preceded it. Post-statehood Hawai'i was not the dreamland of opportunity that my father's generation assumed. Corrupt electoral politics represented a collaborationist elite who, like the previous missionary party, looked to economic exploitation of Hawai'i and our Native culture to advance their power. Tourism came to replace sugar plantations, opening the floodgates to nearly seven million tourists a year from America, Japan, and Europe. Now, a hundred years since the overthrow of our Native government, the spirit and bounty of my ancestral home have been plundered beyond imagining. Our Hawaiian people have been further marginalized, our living conditions and general health diminished, our lands developed and poisoned.

But in 1970, as if announced by oracle, voices of resistance and protest began to be heard from one end of our archipelago to the other. Beginning with anti-development struggles, the poorest and the least articulate began to stand firm against evictions, gathering up their courage to occupy trust lands abused by the military and the state, asserting the primacy of Native language as a form of sovereignty. Now, after twenty years, land rights have been encompassed by a push for self-determination.

And on the front lines, in the glare of public disapproval, are our women—articulate, fierce, and culturally grounded. A great coming together of women's *mana* has given birth to a new form of power based on a traditional Hawaiian belief: women asserting their leadership for the sake of the nation. As I speak to you, at this very moment, nationalist women leaders are organizing and leading our people, even if that entails opposition to our Hawaiian men's leadership in the electoral system, and in the movement.

While Hawaiian men have come to achieve their own place in the legislature and in the governor's office, Hawaiian female leadership has come to the fore in the sovereignty movement. Of course, this is not to say there are no male leaders in our movement. But they are not the most visible, the most articulate, nor the most creative. By any standard—public, personal, political—our sovereignty movement is led by women.

Part of the reason for this is simply colonialism: men are rewarded, including Native men, for collaboration. Women's role, if they are to be collaborators, is not to wield political power but to serve as an adjunct to men who do. Thus, our Native men have something to sell out for, our Native women do not.

But I believe the main reason women lead the nationalist front today is simply that women have not lost sight of the *lāhui*, that is, of the nation. Caring for the nation is, in Hawaiian belief, an extension of caring for the family, the large family that includes both our lands and our people. Our mother is our land, *Papa-hanaumoku*—she who births the islands. This means that Hawaiian women leaders are genealogically empowered to lead the nation.

Genealogy, however, is not a sufficient condition for leadership. A cursory glance at some of our highest-ranking Native women and what they have chosen to do with their lives is a simple way of dispelling the notion that genealogy *determines* leadership, or even *mana*. While our cultural genealogy is as protectors of the earth, our specific genealogies may carry *ali'i* rank. And while *ali'i* rank does play some part in reinforcing leadership, it is insufficient by itself to establish leadership.

No, the defining characteristic of leadership is *mana*, the ability to speak for the people and the land, to command respect by virtue of this ability, and to set the issues of public debate as those which benefit the *lāhui*. In formulating the sovereignty position, Hawaiian women have demonstrated most forcefully what *pono* leadership might be.

Predictably, none of our nationalist women leaders holds an elected political office, a reality that underscores their collective rather than individual focus and their mistrust of the American system. All our women leaders are attached to Hawaiian groups, whether political or cultural, and they are consciously aware of their conflict with Western ways. Consequently, when these women speak, they represent not only their groups but the Hawaiian people as *lāhui Hawai'i*. They all speak from their life experience as Hawaiians in defense of Hawaiian culture, the national culture of our people. This stance is often in opposition to elected leaders, including Hawaiian politicians, who are bound to a constituency and to the American government, and who enter politics primarily for personal career advancement and economic gain.

But despite their shared commonalities, these women do not fit easily into a model of women's leadership in our movement. There is not a single mold, or even two molds, from which these women have been cast. In fact, our women leaders are better characterized by their amazing and delightful uniqueness. Their personal and familial biographies as well as their training and talents are as different from each other as that of any randomly chosen individuals.

What they do share is *mana*, exercised on behalf of the people. Where they exercise it—in the dance, in the law, in the protection of burial places, in practicing traditional agriculture—is specific to each woman.

Four such women, whose public recognition has been substantial and whose dedication is unquestioned include Lilikalā Kame'eleihiwa, Native historian, defender of our religion and our language and keeper of our chants; Dana Naone Hall, poet, community organizer, political strategist, and protector of our ancestors' remains at our largest national cemetery at Honokāhua, Maui; LaFrance Kapaka, community organizer, and self sufficiency activist on behalf of traditional forms of planting, harvesting, and distribution of Hawaiian foods; and my sister, Mililani Trask, attorney, political organizer, and elected governor of our nation, *Ka Lāhui Hawai'i*, a native initiative for self-government.

Educated in Western schools whose purpose is forced assimilation into foreign ways, these women have nevertheless resisted physical and psychological and spiritual colonization in a system that is dominated by foreign investment, by local corruption, and by anti-Hawaiian institutions. Disappointing the hopes of anthropologists and politicians who predict our political demise, these women remain magnificently steadfast against the enormous forces of corporate tourism and the organized greed of our local Democratic Party. And they have proven their commitment to protecting our Native heritage on the land, among our families, and in our hearts.

Lest anyone think the personal lives of these women will hold the key to their leadership, let me say that such a perspective is wholly Western, individually-based, and plain wrong. Even knowing the economic class of these women will not explain why or how they have evolved into leadership positions, or why and how they have been able to sustain their opposition.

The answer to such questions lies in their collective experience and identity as Hawaiians with the Hawaiian nation, that is, with our *lāhui*. In other words, no matter how effective colonialism has been in dismembering our culture and our people, it has not managed-yet-to kill all of us, to push all of us out of Hawai'i, to strangle our love for our people and our language and our land.

Our generation has witnessed a phenomenal energy by our women. At one end of our island archipelago, on the island of Kana'i, LaFrance Kapaka is engaged in creating traditional agricultural farms in the teeth of large corporate owners and major tourist developments. At the other end of our archipelago, on the Big Island of Hawai'i, my sister has created a constitutional government with nearly 16,000 members that is presently seeking Congressional recognition as a Native nation on the model of Federally-recognized American Indian nations. In the middle of our island chain, on the lovely island of Maui, Dana Naone Hall is creating community groups dedicated to the protection of our ancestors' remains and our cultural heritage. And Lilikalā Kame'eleihiwa is keeping us connected to our traditions and our history at the University of Hawai'i.

All these women share an identification with our ancestral value of caring for the people and the land. This lifetime stance is not only an opposing force to colonialism; it is a Hawaiian assertion that Hawai'i is *our* place. And we, the genealogical descendants of the land our mother, *will* protect our birthsands for generations to come.

ALLAN BLOOM

THE STUDENT AND
THE UNIVERSITY

LIBERAL EDUCATION

What image does a first-rank college or university present today to a teen-ager leaving home for the first time, off to the adventure of a liberal education? He has four years of freedom to discover himself—a space between the intellectual wasteland he has left behind and the inevitable dreary professional training that awaits him after the baccalaureate. In this short time he must learn that there is a great world beyond the little one he knows, experience the exhilaration of it and digest enough of it to sustain himself in the intellectual deserts he is destined to traverse. He must do this, that is, if he is to have any hope of a higher life. These are the charmed years when he can, if he so chooses, become anything he wishes and when he has the opportunity to survey his alternatives, not merely those current in his time, or provided by careers, but those available to him as a human being. The importance of these years for an American cannot be overestimated. They are civilization's only chance to get to him.

In looking at him we are forced to reflect on what he should learn if he is to be called educated; we must speculate on what the human potential to be fulfilled is. In the specialties we can avoid such speculation, and the avoidance of them is one of specialization's charms. But here it is a simple duty. What are we to teach this person? The answer may not be evident, but to attempt to answer the question is already to philosophize and to begin to educate. Such a concern in itself poses the question of the unity of man and the unity of the sciences. It is childishness to say, as some do, that everyone must be allowed to develop freely, that it is authoritarian to impose a point of view on the student. In that case, why have a university? If the response is "to provide an atmosphere for learning," we come back to our original questions at the second remove. Which atmosphere? Choices and reflection on the reasons for those choices are unavoidable. The university has to stand for something. The practical effects of unwillingness to think positively about the contents of a liberal education are, on the one hand, to ensure that all the vulgarities of the world outside the university will flourish within it, and, on the other, to impose a much harsher and moral illiberal necessity on the student—the one given by the imperial and imperious demands of the specialized disciplines unfiltered by unifying thought.

The university now offers no distinctive visage to the young person. He finds a democracy of the disciplines—which are there either because they are autochthonous or because they wandered in recently to perform some job that was demanded of the university. This democracy is really an anarchy, because there are no recognized rules for citizenship and no legitimate titles to rule. In short there is no vision, nor is there a set of competing visions, of what an educated human being is. The question has disappeared, for to pose it would be a threat to the peace. There is no organization of the sciences, no tree of knowledge. Out of chaos emerges dispiritedness, because it is impossible to make a reasonable choice. Better to give up on liberal education and get on with a specialty in which there is at least a prescribed curriculum and a prospective career. On the way the student can pick up in elective courses a little of whatever is thought to make one cultured. The student gets no intimation that great mysteries might be revealed to him, that new and higher motives of action might be discovered within him, that a different and more human way of life can be harmoniously constructed by what he is going to learn.

Simply, the university is not distinctive. Equality for us seems to culminate in the unwillingness and incapacity to make claims of superiority, particularly in the domains in which such claims have always been made—art, religion and philosophy. When Weber[1] found that he could not choose between certain high opposites—reason vs. revelation, Buddha vs. Jesus—he did not conclude that all things are equally good, that the distinction between high and low disappears. As a matter of fact he intended to revitalize the consideration of these great alternatives in showing that gravity and danger involved in choosing among them; they were to be heightened in contrast to the trivial considerations of modern life that threatened to overgrow and render indistinguishable the profound problems the confrontation with which makes the bow of the soul taut. The serious intellectual life was for him the battleground of the great decisions, all of which are spiritual or "value" choices. One can no longer present this or that particular view of the educated or civilized man as authoritative; therefore, one must say that education consists in knowing, really knowing, the small number of such views in their integrity. This distinction between profound and superficial—which takes the place of good and bad, true and false—provided a focus for serious study, but it hardly held out against the naturally relaxed democratic tendency to say, "Oh, what's the use?" The first university disruptions at Berkeley were explicitly directed against the multiversity smorgasbord and, I must confess, momentarily and partially engaged my sympathies. It may have even been the case that there was some small element of longing for an education in the motivation of those students. But nothing was done to guide or inform their energy, and the result was merely to add multilife-styles to multidisciplines, the diversity of perversity to the diversity of specialization. What we see so often happening in general happened here too; the insistent demand for greater community ended in greater isolation. Old agreements, old habits, old traditions were not so easily replaced.

Thus, when a student arrives at the university, he finds a bewildering variety of departments and a bewildering variety of courses. And there is no official guidance, no university-wide agreement, about what he *should*

---

1. *Weber*: Max Weber (1864-1920), German social scientist and author of *The Protestant ethic and the Spirit of Capitalism*

study. Nor does he usually find readily available examples, either among students or professors, of a unified use of the university's resources. It is easiest simply to make a career choice and go about getting prepared for that career. The programs designed for those having made such a choice render their student immune to charms that might lead them out of the conventionally respectable. The sirens sing *sotto voce* these days, and the young already have enough wax in their ears[2] to pass them by without danger. These specialties can provide enough courses to take up most of their time for four years in preparation for the inevitable graduate study. With the few remaining courses they can do what they please, taking a bit of this and a bit of that. No public career these days—not doctor nor a lawyer nor politician nor journalist nor businessman nor entertainer—has much to do with humane learning. An education, other than purely professional or technical, can even seem to be an impediment. That is why a countervailing atmosphere in the university would be necessary for the students to gain a taste for intellectual pleasures and learn that they are viable.

The real problem is those students who come hoping to find out what career they want to have, or are simply looking for an adventure with themselves. There are plenty of things for them to do—courses and disciplines enough to spend many a lifetime on. Each department or great division of the university makes a pitch for itself, and each offers a course of study that will make the student an initiate. But how to choose among them? How do they relate to one another? The fact is they do not address one another. They are competing and contradictory, without being aware of it. The problem of the whole is urgently indicated by the very existence of the specialties, but it is never systematically posed. The net effect of the student's encounter with the college catalogue is bewilderment and very often demoralization. It is just a matter of chance whether he finds one or two professors who can give him an insight into one of the great visions of education that have been the distinguishing part of every civilized nation. Most professors are specialists, concerned only with their own

---

2. *wax in their ears*: an allusion to Homer's *Odyssey*, in which the hero, Odysseus, orders his sailors to put wax in their ears to escape the seductive song of the Sirens

fields, interested in the advancement of those fields in their own terms, or in their own personal advancement in a world where all the rewards are on the side of professional distinction. They have been entirely emancipated from the old structure of the university, which at least helped to indicate that they are incomplete, only parts of an unexamined and undiscovered whole. So the student must navigate among a collection of carnival barkers, each trying to lure him into a particular sideshow. This undecided student is an embarrassment to most universities, because he seems to be saying, "I am a whole human being. Help me to form myself in my wholeness and let me develop my real potential," and he is the one to whom they have nothing to say.

Cornell was, as in so many other things, in advance of its time on this issue. The six-year Ph.D. program, richly supported by the Ford Foundation, was directed specifically to high school students who had already made "a firm career choice" and was intended to rush them through to the start of those careers. A sop was given to desolate humanists in the form of money to fund seminars that these young careerists could take on their way through the College of Arts and Sciences. For the rest, the educators could devote their energies to arranging and packaging the program without having to provide it with any substance. That kept them busy enough to avoid thinking about the nothingness of their endeavor. This has been the preferred mode of not looking the Beast in the Jungle in the face, structure not content. The Cornell plan for dealing with the problem of liberal education was to suppress the students' longing for liberal education by encouraging their professionalism and their avarice, providing money and all the prestige the university had available to make careerism the centerpiece of the university.

The Cornell plan dared not state the radical truth, a well-kept secret: the colleges do not have enough to teach their students, not enough to justify keeping them four years, probably not even three years. If the focus is careers, there is hardly one specialty, outside the hardest of the hard natural sciences; which requires more than two years of preparatory training prior to graduate studies. The rest is just wasted time or a period of ripening until the students are old enough for graduate studies. For many graduate careers, even less is really necessary. It is amazing how many undergraduates are poking around for courses to take, without any plan or question to ask, just filling up their college years. In fact, with rare exceptions, the courses are parts of specialties and not designed for general cultivation, or to investigate questions important for human beings as such. The so-called knowledge explosion and increasing specialization have not filled up the college years but emptied them. Those years are impediments; one wants to get beyond them. And, in general, the persons one finds in the professions need not have gone to college, if one is to judge by their tastes, their fund of learning or their interests. They might well have spent their college years in the Peace Corps or the like. These great universities—which can split the atom, find cures for the most terrible diseases, conduct surveys of whole populations and produce massive dictionaries of lost languages—cannot generate a modest program of general education for undergraduate students. This is a parable for our times.

There are attempts to fill the vacuum painlessly with various kinds of fancy packaging of what is already there—study abroad options, individualized majors, etc. Then there are Black Studies and Women's or Gender Studies along with Learn Another Culture. Peace Studies are on their way to a similar prevalence. All this is designed to show that the university is with it and has something in addition to its traditional specialties. The latest item is computer literacy, the full cheapness of which is evident only to those who think a bit about what literacy might mean. It would make some sense to promote literacy literacy, inasmuch as most high school graduates nowadays have difficulty reading and writing. And some institutions are quietly undertaking this worthwhile task. But they do not trumpet the fact, because this is merely a high school function that our current sad state of educational affairs has thrust upon them, about which they are not inclined to boast.

Now that the distractions of the sixties are over, and undergraduate education has become more important again (because the graduate departments, aside from the professional schools, are in trouble due to the shortage of academic jobs), university officials have had somehow to deal with the undeniable fact that the students who enter are uncivilized, and that the universities have some responsibility for civilizing them. If one were to give a base interpretation of the schools' motives, one could allege that their concern stems from shame and self-interest. It is becoming all too evident that liberal education—which is what the small band of prestigious institutions are supposed to provide, in contrast to the big state schools, which are thought simply to prepare specialists to meet the practical demands of a complex society—has no content, that a certain kind of fraud is being perpetrated. For a time the great moral consciousness alleged to have been fostered in students by the great universities, especially their vocation as gladiators who fight war and racism, seemed to fulfill the demands of the collective university conscience. They were doing something other than offering preliminary training for doctors and lawyers. Concern and compassion were thought to be the indefinable X that pervaded all the parts of the Arts and Sciences campus. But when that evanescent mist dissipated during the seventies, and the faculties found themselves face to face with ill-educated young people with no intellectual tastes—unaware that there even are such things, obsessed with getting on with their careers before having looked at life—and the universities offered no counterpoise, no alternative goals, a reaction set in.

Liberal education—since it has for so long been ill-defined, has none of the crisp clarity or institutionalized prestige of the professions, but nevertheless perseveres and has money and respectability connected with it—has always been a battleground for those who are somewhat eccentric in relation to the specialties. It is in something like the condition of churches as opposed to, say, hospitals. Nobody is quite certain of what the religious institutions are supposed to do anymore, but they do have some kind of role either responding to a real human need or as the vestige of what was once a need, and they invite the exploitation of quacks, adventurers, cranks and fanatics. But they also solicit the warmest and most valiant efforts of persons of peculiar gravity and depth. In liberal education, too, the worst and the best fight it out, fakers vs. authentics, sophists vs. philosophers, for the favor of pubic opinion and for control over the study of man in our times. The most conspicuous participants in the struggle are administrators who are formally responsible for presenting some kind of public image of the education their colleges offer, persons with a political agenda or vulgarizers of what the specialties know, and real teachers of the humane disciplines who actually see their relation to the whole and urgently wish to preserve the awareness of it in their students' consciousness.

So, just as in the sixties universities were devoted to removing requirements, in the eighties they are busy with attempts to put them back in, a much more difficult task. The word of the day is "core." It is generally agreed that "we went a bit far in the sixties," and that a little fine-tuning has now become clearly necessary.

There are two typical responses to the problem. The easiest and most administratively satisfying solution is to make use of what is already there in the autonomous departments and simply force the students to cover the fields, i.e., take one or more courses in each of the general divisions of the university: natural science, social science and the humanities. the reigning ideology here is *breadth*, as was *openness* in the age of laxity. The courses are almost always the already existing introductory courses, which are of least interest to the major professors and merely assume the worth and reality of that which is to be studied. It is general education, in the sense in which a jack-of-all-trades is a generalist. He knows a bit of everything and is inferior to the specialist in each area. Students may wish to sample a variety of fields, and it may be good to encourage them to look around and see if there is something that attracts them in one of which they have no experience. But this is not a liberal education and does not satisfy any longing they have for one. It just teaches that there is no high-level generalism, and that what they are doing is preliminary to the real stuff and part of the childhood they are leaving behind. Thus they desire to get it over with and get on with what their professors do seriously. Without recognition of important questions of common concern, there cannot be serious liberal eduction, and attempts to establish it will be but failed gestures.

It is a more or less precise awareness of the inadequacy of this approach to core curricula that motivates the second approach, which consists of what one might call composite courses. There are constructions developed especially for general-education purposes and usually require collaboration of professors drawn from several departments. These courses have titles like "Man in Nature," "War and Moral Responsibility," "The Arts and Creativity,"

"Culture and the Individual." Everything, of course, depends upon who plans them and who teaches them. They have the clear advantage of requiring some reflection on the general needs of students and force specialized professors to broaden their perspectives, at least for a moment. The dangers are trendiness, mere popularization and lack of substantive rigor. In general, the natural scientists do not collaborate in such endeavors, and hence these courses tend to be unbalanced. In short, they do not point beyond themselves and do not provide the student with independent means to pursue permanent questions independently, as, for example, the study of Aristotle or Kant as wholes once did. They tend to be bits of this and that. Liberal education should give the student the sense that learning must and can be both synoptic and precise. For this, a very small, detailed problem can be the best way, if it is framed so as to open out on the whole. Unless the course has the specific intention to lead to the permanent questions, to make the student aware of them and give him some competence in the important works that treat of them, it tends to be a pleasant diversion and a dead end—because it has nothing to do with any program of further study he can imagine. If such programs engage the best energies of the best people in the university, they can be beneficial and provide some of the missing intellectual excitement for both professors and students. But they rarely do, and they are too cut off from the top, from what the various faculties see as their real business. Where the power is determines the life of the whole body. And the intellectual problems unresolved at the top cannot be resolved administratively below. The problem is the lack of any unity of the sciences and the loss of the will or the means even to discuss the issue. The illness above is the cause of the illness below, to which all the good-willed efforts of honest liberal educationists can at best be palliatives.

Of course, the only serious solution is the one that is almost universally rejected: the good old Great Books approach, in which a liberal education means reading certain generally recognized classic texts, just reading them, letting them dictate what the questions are and the method of approaching them—not forcing them into categories we make up, not treating them as historical products, but trying to read them as their author wished them to be read. I am perfectly well aware of, and actually agree with, the objections to the Great Books cult. It is amateurish; it encourages an autodidact's self-assurance without competence; one cannot read all the Great Books carefully; if one only reads Great Books, one can never know what a great, as opposed to an ordinary, book is; there is no way of determining who is to decide what a Great Book or what the canon is; books are made the ends and not the means; the whole movement has a certain coarse evangelistic tone that is the opposite of good taste; it engenders a spurious intimacy with greatness; and so forth. But one thing is certain: wherever the Great Books make up a central part of the curriculum, the students are excited and satisfied, feel they are doing something that is independent and fulfilling, getting something from the university they cannot get elsewhere. The very fact of this special experience, which leads nowhere beyond itself, provides them with a new alternative and a respect for study itself. The advantage they get is an awareness of the classic—particularly important for our innocents; an acquaintance with what big questions were when there were still big questions; models, at the very least, of how to go about answering them; and, perhaps most important of all, a fund of shared experiences and thoughts on which to ground their friendships with one another. Programs based upon judicious use of great texts provide the royal road to students' hearts. Their gratitude at learning of Achilles or the categorical imperative is boundless. Alexandre Koyré, the late historian of science, told me that his appreciation for America was great when—in the first course he taught at the University of Chicago, in 1940 at the beginning of his exile—a student spoke in his paper of Mr. Aristotle, unaware that he was not a contemporary. Koyré said that only an American could have the naive profundity to take Aristotle as living thought, unthinkable for most scholars. A good program of liberal education feeds the student's love of truth and passion to live a good life. It is the easiest thing in the world to devise courses of study, adapted to the particular conditions of each university, which thrill those who take them. The difficulty is in getting them accepted by the faculty.

None of the three great parts of the contemporary university is enthusiastic about the Great Books approach to education. The natural scientists are benevolent toward other fields and toward liberal education, if it does not steal away their students and does not take too much time from their preparatory studies. But they themselves are interested primarily in the solution of the questions now important in their disciplines and are not particularly concerned with discussions for their foundations, inasmuch as they are so evidently successful. They are indifferent to Newtons' conception of time or his disputes with Leibniz about calculus; Aristotle's teleology is an absurdity beneath consideration. Scientific progress, they believe, no longer depends on the kind of comprehensive reflection given to the nature of science by men like Bacon, Descartes, Hume, Kant and Marx. This is merely historical study, and for a long time now, even the greatest scientist have given up thinking about Galileo and Newton. Progress in undoubted. The difficulties about the truth of science raised by positivism, and those about the goodness of science raised by Rousseau and Nietzche, have not really penetrated to the center of scientific consciousness. Hence, no Great Books, but incremental progress, is the theme for them.

Social scientists are in general hostile, because the classic texts tend to deal with the human things the social sciences deal with, and they are very proud of having freed themselves from the shackles of such earlier thought to become truly scientific. And, unlike the natural scientists, they are insecure enough about their achievement to feel threatened by the works of earlier thinkers, perhaps a bit afraid that students will be seduced and fall back into the bad old ways. Moreover, with the possible exception of Weber and Freud, there are no social science books that can be said to be classic. This may be interpreted favorably to the social sciences by comparing them to the natural sciences, which can be said to be a living organism developing by the addition of little cells, a veritable body of knowledge proving itself to be such by the very fact of this almost unconscious growth, with thousands of parts oblivious to the whole, nevertheless contributing to it. This is in opposition to a work of imagination or of philosophy, where a single creator makes and surveys an artificial whole. But whether one interprets the absence of the classic in the social sciences in ways flattering or unflattering to them, the fact causes social scientists discomfort. I remember the professor who taught the introductory graduate course in social science methodology, a famous historian, responding scornfully and angrily to a question I naively put to him about Thucydides with "Thucydides was a fool!"

More difficult to explain is the tepid reaction of humanists to Great Books education, inasmuch as these books now belong almost exclusively to what are called the humanities. One would think that high esteem for the classic would reinforce the spiritual power of the humanities, at a time when their temporal power is at its lowest. And it is true that the most active proponents of liberal education and the study of classic texts are indeed usually humanists. But there is division among them. Some humanities disciplines are just crusty specialties that, although they depend on the status of classic books for their existence, are not really interested in them in their natural state—much philology, for example, is concerned with the languages but not what is said in them—and will and can do nothing to support their own infrastructure. Some humanities disciplines are eager to join the real sciences and transcend their roots in the now overcome mythic past. Some humanists make the legitimate complaints about lack of competence in the teaching and learning of Great Books, although their criticism is frequently undermined by the fact that they are only defending recent scholarly interpretation of the classics rather than a vital, authentic understanding. In their reaction there is a strong element of specialist's jealousy and narrowness. Finally, a large part of the story is just the general debilitation of the humanities, which is both symptom and cause of our present condition.

To repeat, the crisis of liberal education is a reflection of a crisis at the peaks of learning, an incoherence and incompatibility among the first principles with which we interpret the world, an intellectual crisis of the greatest magnitude, which constitutes the crisis of our civilization. But perhaps it would be true to say that the crisis consists not so much in this incoherence but in our incapacity to discuss or even recognize it. Liberal education nourished when it prepared the way for the discussion of a unified view of nature and man's place in it, which the best minds debated on the highest level. It decayed when what lay beyond it were only specialties, the premises of which do not lead to any such vision. The highest is the partial intellect; there is no synopsis.

JEFFREY HART

HOW TO GET A
COLLEGE EDUCATION

I t was in the fall term of 1988 that the truth burst in upon me that something had gone terribly wrong in higher education. It was like the anec-
dote in Auden where the guest at a garden party, sensing something amiss,
suddenly realizes that there is a corpse on the tennis court.

As a professor at Dartmouth, my hours had been taken up with my own
writing, and with teaching a variety of courses—a yearly seminar, a yearly
freshman composition course (which—some good news—all senior professors in the Dartmouth English Department are required to teach), and
courses in my eighteenth-century specialty. Oh, I knew that the larger curriculum lacked shape and purpose, that something was amiss; but I deferred
thinking about it.

Yet there does come that moment.

It came for me in the freshman composition course. The students were
required to write essays based upon assigned reading—in this case, some
Frost poems, Hemingway's *In Our Time, Hamlet*. Then, almost on a whim, I
assigned the first half of Allan Bloom's new surprise best-seller *The Closing
of the American Mind*.

When the time came to discuss the Bloom book, I asked them what they
thought of it.

They hated it.

Oh, yes, they understood perfectly well what Bloom was saying: that they were ignorant, that they believed in clichés, that their education so far had been dangerous piffle and that what they were about to receive was not likely to be any better.

No wonder they hated it. After all, they were the best and the brightest, Ivy Leaguers with stratospheric SAT scores, the Masters of the Universe. Who is Bloom? What is the University of Chicago, anyway?

So I launched into an impromptu oral quiz.

Could anyone (in that class of 25 students) say anything about the Mayflower Compact?

Complete silence.

John Locke?

Nope.

James Madison?

Silentia.

Magna Carta? The Spanish Armada? The Battle of Yorktown? The Bull Moose party? *Don Giovanni*? William James? The Tenth Amendment?

Zero. Zilch. Forget it.

The embarrassment was acute, but some good came of it. The better students, ashamed that their first 12 years of schooling had mostly been wasted (even if they had gone to Choate or Exeter), asked me to recommend some books. I offered such solid things as Samuel Eliot Morison's *Oxford History of the United States*, Max Farrand's *The Framing of the Constitution*, Jacob Burckhardt's *The Civilization of the Renaissance in Italy*. Several students asked for an informal discussion group, and so we started reading a couple of Dante's Cantos per week, Dante being an especially useful author because he casts his net so widely—the ancient world, the (his) modern world, theology, history, ethics.

I quickly became aware of the utter bewilderment of entering freshmen. They emerge from the near-nullity of K-12 and stroll into the chaos of the Dartmouth curriculum, which is embodied in a course catalogue about as large as a telephone directory.

Sir, what courses should I take?

A college like Dartmouth—or Harvard, Princeton, etc.—has requirements so broadly defined that almost anything goes for degree credit. Of course, freshmen are assigned faculty "advisors," but most of them would rather return to the library or the Bunsen burner.

Thus it developed that I began giving an annual lecture to incoming freshmen on the subject, "What Is a College Education? And How to Get One, Even at Dartmouth."

One long-term reason why the undergraduate curriculum at Dartmouth and all comparable institutions is in chaos is specialization. Since World War II, success as a professor has depended increasingly on specialized publication. The ambitious and talented professor is not eager to give introductory or general courses. Indeed, his work has little or nothing to do with undergraduate teaching. Neither Socrates nor Jesus, who published nothing, could possibly receive tenure at a first-line university today.

But in addition to specialization, recent intellectual fads have done extraordinary damage, viz.:

—So-called Post-Modernist thought ("deconstruction," etc.) asserts that one "text" is as much worth analyzing as any other, whether it be a movie, a comic book, or Homer. The lack of a "canon" of important works leads to course offerings in, literally, anything.

—"Affirmative Action" is not just a matter of skewed admissions and hiring, but also a mentality or ethos. That is, if diversity is more important than quality in admissions and hiring, why should it not be so in the curriculum? Hence the courses in things like Nicaraguan Lesbian Poetry.

—Concomitantly, ideology has been imposed on the curriculum to a startling degree. In part this represents a sentimental attempt to resuscitate Marxism, with assorted Victim Groups standing in for the old Proletariat; in part it is a new Identity Politics in which being Black, Lesbian, Latino, Homosexual, Radical Feminist, and so forth takes precedence over any scholarly pursuit. These Victimologies are usually presented as "Studies" programs outside the regular departments, so as to avoid the usual academic standards. Yet their course offerings carry degree credit.

On an optimistic note, I think that most or all of Post-Modernism, the Affirmative Action/Multicultural ethos, and the Victimologies will soon pass from the scene. The great institutions have a certain sense of self-preservation. Harvard almost lost its Law School to a Marxist faculty faction, but then cleaned house. Tenure will keep the dead men walking for another twenty years or so, but then we will have done with them.

But for the time being, what these fads have done to the liberal-arts and social-sciences curriculum since around 1968 is to clutter it with all sorts of nonsense, nescience, and distraction. The entering student needs to be wary lest he waste his time and his parents' money and come to consider all higher education an outrageous fraud. The good news is that the wise student can still get a college education today, even at Dartmouth, Harvard, Yale, and Princeton.

Of course the central question is one of *telos*, or goal. What is the liberal-arts education supposed to produce? Once you have the answer to this question, course selection becomes easy.

I mean to answer that question here. But first, I find that undergraduates and their third-mortgaged parents appreciate some practical tips, such as:

Select the "ordinary" courses. I use *ordinary* here in a paradoxical and challenging way. An *ordinary* course is one that has always been taken and obviously should be taken—even if the student is not yet equipped with a sophisticated rationale for so doing. The student should be discouraged from putting his money on the cutting edge of interdisciplinary cross-textuality.

Thus, do take American and European history, an introduction to philosophy, American and European literature, the Old and New Testaments, and at least one modern language. It would be absurd not to take a course in Shakespeare, the best poet in our language. There is art and music history. The list can be expanded, but these areas every educated person should have a decent knowledge of—with specialization coming later on.

I hasten to add that I applaud the student who devotes his life to the history of China or Islam, but that too should come later. America is part of the narrative of European history.

If the student should seek out those "ordinary" courses, then it follows that he should avoid the flashy come-ons. Avoid things like Nicaraguan Lesbian Poets. Yes, and anything listed under "Studies," any course whose description uses the words "interdisciplinary," "hegemonic," "phallocratic," or "empowerment," anything that mentions "keeping a diary," any course with a title like "Adventures in Film."

Also, any male professor who comes to class without a jacket and tie should be regarded with extreme prejudice unless he has won a Nobel Prize.

All these are useful rules of thumb. A theoretical rationale for a liberal-arts education, however, derives from that *telos* mentioned above. What is such an education supposed to produce?

A philosophy professor I studied with as an undergraduate had two phrases he repeated so often that they stay in the mind, a technique made famous by Matthew Arnold.

He would say, *"History must be told."*

History, he explained, is to a civilization what memory is to an individual, an irreducible part of identity.

He also said, *"The goal of education is to produce the citizen."* He defined the citizen as the person who, if need be, could re-create his civilization.

Now, it is said that Goethe was the last man who knew all the aspects of his civilization (I doubt that he did), but that after him things became too complicated. My professor had something different in mind. He meant that the citizen should know the great themes of his civilization, its important areas of thought, its philosophical and religious controversies, the outline of its history and its major works. The citizen need not know quantum physics, but he should know that it is there and what it means. Once the citizen knows the shape, the narrative, of his civilization, he is able to locate new things—and other civilizations—in relation to it.

The narrative of Western civilization can be told in different ways, but a useful paradigm has often been called "Athens and Jerusalem." Broadly construed, "Athens" means a philosophical and scientific view of actuality and "Jerusalem" a spiritual and scriptural one. The working out of Western civilization represents an interaction—tension, fusion, conflict—between the two.

Both Athens and Jerusalem have a heroic, or epic, phase. For Athens, the Homeric poems are a kind of scripture, the subject of prolonged ethical meditation. In time the old heroic ideals are internalized as heroic philosophy in Socrates, Plato, and Aristotle.

For Jerusalem, the heroic phase consists of the Hebrew narratives. Here again, a process of internalization occurs, Jesus internalizing the Mosaic

Law. Socrates is the heroic philosopher, Jesus the ideal of heroic holiness, both new ideals in their striking intensity.

During the first century of the Christian Era, Athens and Jerusalem converge under the auspices of Hellenistic thought, most notably in Paul and in John, whose gospel defined Jesus by using the Greek term for order, *Logos*.

Athens and Jerusalem were able to converge, despite great differences, because in some ways they overlap. The ultimate terms of Socrates and Plato, for example, cannot be entirely derived from reason. The god of Plato and Aristotle is monotheistic, though still the god of the philosophers. Yet Socrates considers that his rational universe dictates personal immortality.

In the Hebrew epic, there are hints of a law prior to the Law of revelation and derived from reason. Thus, when Abraham argues with God over the fate of Sodom and Gomorrah, Abraham appeals to a known principle of justice which God also assumes.

Thus Athens is not pure reason and Jerusalem not pure revelation. Both address the perennial question of why there is something rather than nothing.

From the prehistoric figures in Homer and in Genesis—Achilles, Abraham—the great conversation commences. Thucydides and Virgil seek order in history. St. Augustine tries to synthesize Paul and Platonism. Montaigne's skepticism would never have been articulated without a prior assertion of cosmic order. Erasmus believed Christianity would prevail if only it could be put in the purest Latin. Shakespeare made a world, and transcended Lear's storm with that final calmed and sacramental Tempest. Rousseau would not have proclaimed the goodness of man if Calvin had not said the opposite. Dante held all the contradictions together in a total structure—for a glorious moment. Kafka could not see beyond the edges of his nightmare, but Dostoyevsky found love just beyond the lowest point of sin. The eighteenth-century men of reason knew the worst, and settled for the luminous stability of a bourgeois republic.

By any intelligible standard the other great civilization was China, yet it lacked the Athens–Jerusalem tension and dynamism. Much more static, its symbols were the Great Wall and the Forbidden City, not

Odysseus/Columbus, Chartres, the Empire State Building, the love that moves the sun and the other stars.

When undergraduates encounter the material of our civilization—that is, the liberal arts—then they know that they are going somewhere. They are becoming citizens.

JEAN ANYON

From SOCIAL CLASS AND THE HIDDEN CURRICULUM OF WORK

Scholars in political economy and the sociology of knowledge have recently argued that public schools in complex industrial societies like our own make available different types of educational experience and curriculum knowledge to students in different social classes. Bowles and Gintis[1] for example, have argued that students in different social-class backgrounds are rewarded for classroom behaviors that correspond to personality traits allegedly rewarded in the different occupational strata—the working classes for docility and obedience, the managerial classes for initiative and personal assertiveness. Basil Bernstein, Pierre Bourdieu, and Michael W. Apple,[2] focusing on school knowledge, have argued that knowledge and skills leading to social power and regard (medical, legal, managerial) are made available to the advantaged social groups but are

Reprinted from *Journal of Education*, Boston University School of Education, 1980, with permission from the Trustees of Boston University and the author.

1. S. Bowles and H. Gintis, Schooling in *Capitalist America: Educational Reform and the Contradictions of Economic Life* (New York: Basic Books, 1976). [Author's note]
2. Bernstein, Class. Codes and Control, Vol. 3. *Towards a Theory of Educational Transmission*, 2d ed. (London: Routledge & Kegan Paul, 1977); P. Bourdieu and J. Passeron, *Reproduction in Education, Society and Culture* (Beverly Hills, Calif.: Sage, 1977); M. W. Apple, *Ideology and Curriculum* (Boston: Routledge & Kegan Paul, 1979). [Author's note]

withheld from the working classes, to whom a more "practical" curriculum is offered (manual skills, clerical knowledge). While there has been considerable argumentation of these points regarding education in England, France, and North America, there has been little or no attempt to investigate these ideas empirically in elementary or secondary schools and classrooms in this country.[3]

This article offers tentative empirical support (and qualification) of the above arguments by providing illustrative examples of differences in student work in classrooms in contrasting social class communities. The examples were gathered as part of an ethnographical[4] study of curricular, pedagogical, and pupil evaluation practices in five elementary schools. The article attempts a theoretical contribution as well and assesses student work in the light of a theoretical approach to social-class analysis. . . . It will be suggested that there is a "hidden curriculum" in schoolwork that has profound implications for the theory—and consequence—of everyday activity in education. . . .

THE SAMPLE OF SCHOOLS

. . . The social-class designation of each of the five schools will be identified, and the income, occupation, and other relevant available social characteristics of the students and their parents will be described. The first three schools are in a medium-sized city district in northern New Jersey, and the other two are in a nearby New Jersey suburb.

The first two schools I will call *working-class schools*. Most of the parents have blue-collar jobs. Less than a third of the fathers are skilled, while the majority are in unskilled or semiskilled jobs. During the period of the study (1978-1979), approximately 15 percent of the fathers were unemployed. The large majority (85 percent) of the families are white. The following occupations are typical: platform, storeroom, and stockroom workers;

---

3. But see, in a related vein, M.W. Apple and N. King, "What Do Schools Teach?" *Curriculum Inquiry* 6 (1977): 341-58; R. C. Rist, *The Urban School: A Factory for Failure* (Cambridge, Mass: MIT Press, 1973). [Author's note]

4. *ethnographical*: Based on an anthropological study of cultures or subcultures—the "cultures" in this case being the five schools observed.

foundrymen, pipe welders, and boilermakers; semiskilled and unskilled assemblyline operatives; gas station attendants, auto mechanics, maintenance workers, and security guards. Less than 30 percent of the women work, some part-time and some full-time, on assembly lines, in storerooms and stockrooms, as waitresses, barmaids, or sales clerks. Of the fifth-grade parents, none of the wives of the skilled workers had jobs. Approximately 15 percent of the families in each school are at or below the federal "poverty" level,[5] most of the rest of the family incomes are at or below $12,000, except some of the skilled workers whose incomes are higher. The incomes of the majority of the families in these two schools (at or below $12,000) are typical of 38.6 percent of the families in the United States.[6]

The third school is called the *middle-class school*, although because of neighborhood residence patterns, the population is a mixture of several social classes. The parents' occupations can be divided into three groups: a small group of blue-collar "rich," who are skilled, well-paid workers such as printers, carpenters, plumbers, and construction workers. The second group is composed of parents in working-class and middle-class white-collar jobs: women in office jobs, technicians, supervisors in industry, and parents employed by the city (such as firemen, policemen, and several of the school's teachers). The third group is composed of occupations such as personnel directors in local firms, accountants, "middle management," and a few small capitalists (owners of shops in the area). The children of several local doctors attend this school. Most family incomes are between $13,000 and $25,000, with a few higher. This income range is typical of 38.9 percent of the families in the United States.[7]

The fourth school has a parent population that is at the upper income level of the upper middle class and is predominantly professional. This

---

5. The U.S. Bureau of the Census defines *poverty* for a nonfarm family of four as a yearly income of $6,191 a year or less. U.S. Bureau of the Census, *Statistical Abstract of the United States*: 1978 (Washington, D.C.: U.S. Government Printing Office, 1978), p. 465, table 754. [Author's note]
6. U.S. Bureau of the Census, "Money Income in 1977 of Families and Persons in the United States," *Current Population Reports Series* P-60, no. 118 (Washington, D.C.: U.S. Government Printing Office, 1979), p.2, table A. [Author's note]
7. Ibid. [Author's note]

school will be called the *affluent professional school*. Typical jobs are cardiologist, interior designer, corporate lawyer or engineer, executive in advertising or television. There are some families who are not as affluent as the majority (the family of the superintendent of the district's schools, and the one or two families in which the fathers are skilled workers). In addition, a few of the families are more affluent than the majority and can be classified in the capitalist class (a partner in a prestigious Wall Street stock brokerage firm). Approximately 90 percent of the children in this school are white. Most family incomes are between $40,000 and $80,000. This income span represents approximately 7 percent of the families in the United States.[8]

In the fifth school the majority of the families belong to the capitalist class. This school will be called the *executive elite school* because most of the fathers are top executives (for example, presidents and vice-presidents) in major United States-based multinational corporations—for example, AT&T, RCA, Citibank, American Express, U.S. Steel. A sizable group of fathers are top executives in financial firms in Wall Street. There are also a number of fathers who list their occupations as "general counsel" to a particular corporation, and these corporations are also among the large multinationals. Many of the mothers do volunteer work in the Junior League, Junior Fortnightly, or other service groups; some are intricately involved in town politics; and some are themselves in well-paid occupations. There are no minority children in the school. Almost all the family incomes are over $100,000, with some in the $500,000 range. The incomes in this school represent less than 1 percent of the families in the United States.[9]

Since each of the five schools is only one instance of elementary education in a particular social class context, I will not generalize beyond the sample. However, the examples of schoolwork which follow will suggest characteristics of education in each social setting that appear to have

---

8. This figure is an estimate. According to the Bureau of the Census, only 2.6 percent of families in the United States have money income of $50,000 or over. U.S. Bureau of the Census, Current Population Reports Series P-60. For figures on income at these higher levels, see J. D. Smith and S. Franklin, "The Concentration of Personal Wealth, 1922-1969, *American Economic Review* 64 (1974): 162~67. [Author's note]

theoretical and social significance and to be worth investigation in a larger number of schools. . . .

THE WORKING-CLASS SCHOOLS

In the two working-class schools, work is following the steps of a procedure. The procedure is usually mechanical, involving rote behavior and very little decision-making or choice. The teachers rarely explain why the work is being assigned, how it might connect to other assignments, or what the idea is that lies behind the procedure or gives it coherence and perhaps meaning or significance. Available textbooks are not always used, and the teachers often prepare their own dittos or put work examples on the board. Most of the rules regarding work are designations of what the children are to do; the rules are steps to follow. These steps are told to the children by the teachers and are often written on the board. The children are usually told to copy the steps as notes. These notes are to be studied. Work is often evaluated not according to whether it is right or wrong but according to whether the children followed the right steps.

The following examples illustrate these points. In math, when two-digit division was introduced, the teacher in one school gave a four-minute lecture on what the terms are called (which number is the divisor, dividend, quotient, and remainder). The children were told to copy these names in their notebooks. Then the teacher told them the steps to follow to do the problems, saying, "This is how you do them." The teacher listed the steps on the board, and they appeared several days later as a chart hung in the middle of the front wall: "Divide, Multiply, Subtract, Bring Down." The children often did examples of two-digit division. When the teacher went over the examples with them, he told them what the procedure was for each problem, rarely asking them to conceptualize or explain it themselves: "Three into twenty-two is seven; do your subtraction and one is left over." During the week that two-digit division was introduced (or at any other time), the investigator did not observe any discussion of the idea of grouping involved in division, any use of manipulables, or any attempt to relate

---

9. Smith and Franklin, "The Concentration of Personal Wealth" [Author's note]

two-digit division to any other mathematical process. Nor was there any attempt to relate the steps to an actual or possible thought process of the children. The observer did not hear the terms *dividend*, *quotient*, and so on, used again. The math teacher in the other working-class school followed similar procedures regarding two-digit division and at one point her class seemed confused. She said, "You're confusing yourselves. You're tensing up. Remember, when you do this, it's the same steps over and over again—and that's the way division always is." Several weeks later, after a test, a group of her children "still didn't get it," and she made no attempt to explain the concept of dividing things into groups or to give them manipulables for their own investigation. Rather, she went over the steps with them again and told them that they "needed more practice."

In other areas of math, work is also carrying out often unexplained fragmented procedures. For example, one of the teachers led the children through a series of steps to make a 1-inch grid on their paper *without* telling them that they were making a 1-inch grid or that it would be used to study scale. She said, "Take your ruler. Put it across the top. Make a mark at every number; Then move your ruler down to the bottom. No, put it across the bottom. Now make a mark on top of every number. Now draw a line from . . ." At this point a girl said that she had a faster way to do it and the teacher said, "No, you don't; you don't even know what I'm making yet. Do it this way or it's wrong." After they had made the lines up and down and across, the teacher told them she wanted them to make a figure by connecting some dots and to measure that, using the scale of 1 inch equals 1 mile. Then they were to cut it out. She said, "Don't cut it until I check it."

In both working-class schools, work in language arts is mechanics of punctuation (commas, periods, question marks, exclamation points), capitalization, and the four kinds of sentences. One teacher explained to me, "Simple punctuation is all they'll ever use." Regarding punctuation, either a teacher or a ditto stated the rules for where, for example, to put commas. The investigator heard no classroom discussion of the aural context of punctuation (which, of course, is what gives each mark its meaning). Nor did the investigator hear any statement or inference that placing a punctuation mark could be a decision-making process, depending, for example, on one's intended meaning. Rather, the children were told to follow the rules. Language arts did not involve creative writing. There were several writing assignments throughout the year, but in each instance the children were given a ditto, and they wrote answers to questions on the sheet. For example, they wrote their "autobiography" by answering such questions as "Where were you born?" "What is your favorite animal?" on a sheet entitled "All About Me."

In one of the working-class schools, the class had a science period several times a week. On the three occasions observed, the children were not called upon to set up experiments or to give explanations for facts or concepts. Rather, on each occasion the teacher told them in his own words what the book said. The children copied the teacher's sentences from the board. Each day that preceded the day they were to do a science experiment, the teacher told them to copy the directions from the book for the procedure they would carry out the next day and to study the list at home that night. The day after each experiment, the teacher went over what they had "found" (they did the experiments as a class, and each was actually a class demonstration led by the teacher). Then the teacher wrote what they "found" on the board, and the children copied that in their notebooks. Once or twice a year there are science projects. The project is chosen and assigned by the teacher from a box of 3-by-5-inch cards. On the card the teacher has written the question to be answered, the books to use, and how much to write. Explaining the cards to the observer, the teacher said, "It tells them exactly what to do, or they couldn't do it."

Social studies in the working-class schools is also largely mechanical, rote work that was given little explanation or connection to larger contexts. In one school, for example, although there was a book available, social studies work was to copy the teacher's notes from the board. Several times a week for a period of several months the children copied these notes. The fifth grades in the district were to study United States history. The teacher used a booklet she had purchased called "The Fabulous Fifty States." Each day she put information from the booklet in outline form on the board and the children copied it. The type of information did not vary: the name of the state, its abbreviation, state capital, nickname of the state, its main products, main business, and a "Fabulous Fact" ("Idaho grew twenty-seven billion potatoes in one year. That's enough potatoes for each man, woman, and . . ."). As the children finished copying the sentences, the teacher erased them and wrote more. Children would occasionally go to the front to pull down the wall map in order to locate the states they were copying, and the teacher did not dissuade them. But the observer never saw her refer to the map; nor did the observer ever hear her make other than perfunctory remarks concerning the information the children were copying. Occasionally the children colored in a ditto and cut it out to make a stand-up figure (representing, for example, a man roping a cow in the Southwest). These were referred to by the teacher as their social studies "projects."

Rote behavior was often called for in classroom work. When going over math and language art skills sheets, for example, as the teacher asked for the answer to each problem, he fired the questions rapidly, staccato, and the scene reminded the observer of a sergeant drilling recruits: above all, the questions demanded that you stay at attention: "The next one? What do I put here? . . . Here? Give us the next." Or "How many commas in this sentence? Where do I put them . . . The next one?"

The four fifth-grade teachers observed in the working-class schools attempted to control classroom time and space by making decisions without consulting the children and without explaining the basis for their decisions. The teacher's control thus often seemed capricious. Teachers, for instance, often ignored the bells to switch classes—deciding among themselves to keep the children after the period was officially over to continue with the work or for disciplinary reasons or so they (the teachers) could stand in the hall and talk. There were no clocks in the rooms in either school, and the children often asked, "What period is this?" "When do we go to gym?" The children had no access to materials. These were handed out by teachers and closely guarded. Things in the room "belonged" to the teacher: "Bob, bring me my garbage can." The teachers continually gave the children orders. Only three times did the investigator hear a teacher in either working class school preface a directive with an unsarcastic "please," or "let's" or "would you." Instead, the teachers said, "Shut up," "Shut your mouth," "Open your books," "Throw your gum away—if you want to rot your teeth, do it on your own time." Teachers made every effort to control the movement of the children, and often shouted, "Why are you out of your seat??!!" If the children got permission to leave the room, they had to take a written pass with the date and time. . . .

MIDDLE-CLASS SCHOOL

In the middle-class school, work is getting the right answer. If one accumulates enough right answers, one gets a good grade. One must follow the directions in order to get the right answers, but the directions often call for some figuring, some choice, some decision-making. For example, the children must often figure out by themselves what the directions ask them to do and how to get the answer: what do you do first, second, and perhaps third? Answers are usually found in books or by listening to the teacher. Answers are usually words, sentences, numbers, or facts and dates; one writes them on paper, and one should be neat. Answers must be given in the right order, and one cannot make them up.

The following activities are illustrative. Math involves some choice: one may do two-digit division the long way or the short way, and there are some math problems that can be done "in your head." When the teacher explains how to do two-digit division, there is recognition that a cognitive process is involved; she gives you several ways and says, "I want to make sure you understand what you're doing—so you get it right"; and, when they go over the homework, she asks the children to tell how they did the problem and what answer they got.

In social studies the daily work is to read the assigned pages in the textbook and to answer the teacher's questions. The questions are almost always designed to check on whether the students have read the assignment and understood it: who did so-and-so; what happened after that; when did it happen, where, and sometimes, why did it happen? The answers are in the book and in one's understanding of the book; the teacher's hints when one doesn't know the answers are to "read it again" or to look at the picture or at the rest of the paragraph. One is to search for the answer in the "context," in what is given.

Language arts is "simple grammar, what they need for everyday life." The language arts teacher says, "They should learn to speak properly, to write business letters and thank-you letters, and to understand what nouns and verbs and simple subjects are." Here, as well, actual work is to choose the right answers, to understand what is given. The teacher often says, "Please read the next sentence and then I'll question you about it." One teacher said in some exasperation to a boy who was fooling around in class, "If you don't know the answers to the questions I ask, then you can't stay in this *class!* [pause] You *never* know the answers to the questions I ask, and it's not fair to me—and certainly not to you!"

Most lessons are based on the textbook. This does not involve a critical perspective on what is given there. For example, a critical perspective in social studies is perceived as dangerous by these teachers because it may lead to controversial topics; the parents might complain. The children, however, are often curious, especially in social studies. Their questions are tolerated and usually answered perfunctorily. But after a few minutes, the teacher will say, "All right, we're not going any farther. Please open your social studies workbook." While the teachers spend a lot of time explaining and expanding on what the textbooks say, there is little attempt to analyze how or why things happen, or to give thought to how pieces of a culture, or, say, a system of numbers or elements of a language fit together or can be analyzed. What has happened in the past and what exists now may not be equitable or fair, but (shrug) that is the way things are and one does not confront such matters in school. For example, in social studies after a child is called on to read a passage about the pilgrims, the teacher summarizes the paragraph and then says, "So you can see how strict they were about everything." A child asks, "Why?" "Well, because they felt that if you weren't busy you'd get into trouble." Another child asks, "Is it true that they burned women at the stake?" The teacher says, "Yes, if a woman did anything strange, they hanged them. [*sic*] What would a woman do, do you think, to make them burn them? [*sic*] See if you can come up with better answers than my other [social studies] class." Several children offer suggestions, to which the teacher nods but does not comment. Then she says, "Okay, good," and calls on the next child to read.

Work tasks do not usually request creativity. Serious attention is rarely given in school work on *how* the children develop or express their own feelings and ideas, either linguistically or in graphic form. On the occasions when creativity or self-expression is requested, it is peripheral to the main activity or it is "enrichment" or "for fun." During a lesson on what similes are, for example, the teacher explains what they are, puts several on the board, gives some other examples herself, and then asks the children if they can "make some up." She calls on three children who give similes, two of which are actually in the book they have open before them. The teacher does not comment on this and then asks several others to choose similes from the list of phrases in the book. Several do so correctly, and she says, "Oh good! You're picking them out! See how good we are?" Their homework is to pick out the rest of the similes from the list.

Creativity is not often requested in social studies and science projects, either. Social studies projects, for example, are given with directions to "find information on your topic" and write it up. The children are not supposed to copy but to "put it in your own words." Although a number of the projects subsequently went beyond the teacher's direction to find information and had quite expressive covers and inside illustrations, the teacher's evaluative comments had to do with the amount of information, whether they had "copied," and if their work was neat.

The style of control of the three fifth-grade teachers observed in this school varied from somewhat easygoing to strict, but in contrast to the working-class schools, the teachers' decisions were usually based on external rules and regulations—for example, on criteria that were known or available to the children. Thus, the teachers always honor the bells for changing classes, and they usually evaluate children's work by what is in the textbooks and answer booklets.

There is little excitement in schoolwork for the children, and the assignments are perceived as having little to do with their interests and feelings. As one child said, what you do is "store facts up in your head like cold storage—

---

10. A dominant feeling, expressed directly and indirectly by teachers in this school, was boredom with their work. They did, however, in contrast to the working-class schools, almost always carry out lessons during class times. [Author's note]

until you need it later for a test or your job." Thus, doing well is important because there are thought to be other likely rewards: a good job or college.[10]

AFFLUENT PROFESSIONAL SCHOOL

In the affluent professional school, work is creative activity carried out independently. The students are continually asked to express and apply ideas and concepts. Work involves individual thought and expressiveness, expansion and illustration of ideas, and choice of appropriate method and material. (The class is not considered an open classroom, and the principal explained that because of the large number of discipline problems in the fifth grade this year they did not departmentalize. The teacher who agreed to take part in the study said she is "more structured" this year than she usually is.) The products of work in this class are often written stories, editorials and essays or representations of ideas in mural, graph, or craft form. The products of work should not be like everybody else's and should show individuality. They should exhibit good design, and (this is important) they must also fit empirical reality. Moreover, one's work should attempt to interpret or "make sense" of reality. The relatively few rules to be followed regarding work are usually criteria for, or limits on, individual activity. One's product is usually evaluated for the quality of its expression and for the appropriateness of its conception to the task. In many cases, one's own satisfaction with the product is an important criterion for its evaluation. When right answers are called for, as in commercial materials like SRA (Science Research Associates) and math, it is important that the children decide on an answer as a result of thinking about the idea involved in what they're being asked to do. Teacher's hints are to "think about it some more."

The following activities are illustrative. The class takes home a sheet requesting each child's parents to fill in the number of cars they have, the number of television sets, refrigerators, games, or rooms in the house, and so on. Each child is to figure the average number of a type of possession owned by the fifth grade. Each child must compile the "data" from all the sheets. A calculator is available in the classroom to do the mechanics of finding the average. Some children decide to send sheets to the fourth-grade families for comparison. Their work should be "verified" by a classmate before it is handed in.

Each child and his or her family has made a geoboard. The teacher asks the class to get their geoboards from the side cabinet, to take a handful of rubber bands, and then to listen to what she would like them to do. She says, "I would like you to design a figure and then find the perimeter and area. When you have it, check with your neighbor. After you've done that, please transfer it to graph paper and tomorrow I'll ask you to make up a question about it for someone. When you hand it in, please let me know whose it is and who verified it. Then I have something else for you to do that's really fun. [pause] Find the average number of chocolate chips in three cookies. I'll give you three cookies, and you'll have to *eat* your way through, I'm afraid!" Then she goes around the room and gives help, suggestions, praise, and admonitions that they are getting noisy. They work sitting, or standing up at their desks, at benches in the back, or on the floor. A child hands the teacher his paper and she comments, "I'm not accepting this paper. Do a better design." To another child she says, "That's fantastic! But you'll never find the area. Why don't you draw a figure inside [the big one] and subtract to get the area?"

The school district requires the fifth grade to study ancient civilization (in particular, Egypt, Athens, and Sumer). In this classroom, the emphasis is on illustrating and re-creating the culture of the people of ancient times. The following are typical activities: the children made an 8mm film on Egypt, which one of the parents edited. A girl in the class wrote the script, and the class acted it out. They put the sound on themselves. They read stories of those days. They wrote essays and stories depicting the lives of the people and the societal and occupational divisions. They chose from a list of projects, all of which involved graphic representations of ideas: for example, "Make a mural depicting the division of labor in Egyptian society."

Each child wrote and exchanged a letter in hieroglyphics with a fifth grader in another class, and they also exchanged stories they wrote in cuneiform. They made a scroll and singed the edges so it looked authentic. They each chose an occupation and made an Egyptian plaque representing that occupation, simulating the appropriate Egyptian design. They carved their design on a cylinder of wax, pressed the wax into clay, and then baked the clay. Although one girl did not choose an occupation but carved instead a series of gods and slaves, the teacher said, "That's all right, Amber, it's beautiful." As they were working the teacher said, "Don't cut into your clay until you're satisfied with your design."

Social studies also involves almost daily presentation by the children of some event from the news. The teacher's questions ask the children to expand what they say, to give more details, and to be more specific. Occasionally she adds some remarks to help them see connections between events.

The emphasis on expressing and illustrating ideas in social studies is accompanied in language arts by an emphasis on creative writing. Each child wrote a rebus story for a first grader whom they had interviewed to see what kind of story the child liked best. They wrote editorials on pending decisions by the school board and radio plays, some of which were read over the school intercom from the office and one of which was performed in the auditorium. There is no language arts textbook because, the teacher said, "The principal wants us to be creative." There is not much grammar, but there is punctuation. One morning when the observer arrived, the class was doing a punctuation ditto. The teacher later apologized for using the ditto. "It's just for review," she said. "I don't teach punctuation that way. We use their language." The ditto had three unambiguous rules for where to put commas in a sentence. As the teacher was going around to help the children with the ditto, she repeated several times, "Where you put commas depends on how you say the sentence; it depends on the situation and what you want to say." Several weeks later the observer saw another punctuation activity. The teacher had printed a five-paragraph story on an oak tag and then cut it into phrases. She read the whole story to the class from the book, then passed out the phrases. The group had to decide how the phrases could best be put together again. (They arranged the phrases on the door.) The point was not to replicate the story, although that was not irrelevant, but to "decide what you think the best way is." Punctuation marks on cardboard pieces were then handed out, and the children discussed and then decided what mark was best at each place they thought one was needed. At the end of each paragraph the teacher asked, "Are you satisfied with the way the paragraphs are now? Read it to yourself and see how it sounds." Then she read the original story again, and they compared the two.

X Describing her goals in science to the investigator, the teacher said, "We use ESS (Elementary Science Study). It's very good because it gives a hands-on experience—so they can make *sense* out of it. It doesn't matter whether it [what they find] is right or wrong. I bring them together and there's value in discussing their ideas."

The products of work in this class are often highly valued by the children and the teacher. In fact, this was the only school in which the investigator was not allowed to take original pieces of the children's work for her files. If the work was small enough, however, and was on paper, the investigator could duplicate it on the copying machine in the office.

X The teacher's attempt to control the class involves constant negotiation. She does not give direct orders unless she is angry because the children have been too noisy. Normally, she tries to get them to foresee the consequences of their actions and to decide accordingly. For example, lining them up to go see a play written by the sixth graders, she says, "I presume you're lined up by someone with whom you want to sit. I hope you're lined up by someone you won't get in trouble with." . . .

One of the few rules governing the children's movement is that no more than three children may be out of the room at once. There is a school rule that anyone can go to the library at any time to get a book. In the fifth grade I observed, they sign their name on the chalkboard and leave. There are no passes. X Finally, the children have a fair amount of officially sanctioned say over what happens in the class. For example, they often negotiate what work is to be done. If the teacher wants to move on to the next subject, but the children say they are not ready, they want to work on their present projects some more, she very often lets them do it.

EXECUTIVE ELITE SCHOOL

In the executive elite school, work is developing one's analytical intellectual powers. Children are continually asked to reason through a problem, to produce intellectual products that are both logically sound and of top academic quality. A primary goal of thought is to conceptualize rules by which elements may fit together in systems and then to apply these rules in solving a problem. Schoolwork helps one to achieve, to excel, to prepare for life.

The following are illustrative. The math teacher teaches area and perimeter by having the children derive formulas for each. First she helps them, through discussion at the board, to arrive at A = W x L as a formula (not the formula) for area. After discussing several, she says, "Can anyone make up a formula for perimeter? Can you figure that out yourselves? [pause] Knowing what we know, can we think of a formula?" She works out three children's suggestions at the board, saying to two, "Yes, that's a good one," and then asks the class if they can think of any more. No one volunteers. To prod them, she says, "If you use rules and good reasoning, you get many ways. Chris, can you think up a formula?"

She discusses two-digit division with the children as a decision-making process. Presenting a new type of problem to them, she asks, "What's the first decision you'd make if presented with this kind of example? What is the first thing you'd *think*? Craig?" Craig says, "To find my first partial quotient. She responds, "Yes, that would be your first decision. How would you do that?" Craig explains, and then the teacher says, "OK, we'll see how that works for you." The class tries his way. Subsequently, she comments on the merits and shortcomings of several other children's decisions. Later, she tells the investigator that her goals in math are to develop their reasoning and mathematical thinking and that, unfortunately, "there's no *time* for manipulables."

While right answers are important in math, they are not "given" by the book or by the teacher but may be challenged by the children. Going over some problems in late September the teacher says, "Raise your hand if you do not agree." A child says, "I don't agree with sixty-four." The teacher responds, "OK, there's a question about sixty-four. [to class] Please check it. Owen, they're disagreeing with you. Kristen, they're checking yours." The teacher emphasized this repeatedly during September and October with statements like "Don't be afraid to say you disagree. In the last [math] class, somebody disagreed, and they were right. Before you disagree, check yours, and if you still think we're wrong, then we'll check it out." By Thanksgiving, the children did not often speak in terms of right and wrong math problems but of whether they agreed with the answer that had been given.

There are complicated math mimeos with many word problems. Whenever they go over the examples, they discuss how each child has set up the problem. The children must explain it precisely. On one occasion the teacher said, "I'm more—just as interested in *how* you set up the problem as in what answer you find. If you set up a problem in a good way, the answer is *easy* to find."

Social studies work is most often reading and discussion of concepts and independent research. There are only occasional artistic, expressive, or illustrative projects. Ancient Athens and Sumer are, rather, societies to analyze. The following questions are typical of those that guide the children's independent research. "What mistakes did Pericles make after the war?" "What mistakes did the citizens of Athens make?" "What are the elements of a civilization?" "How did Greece build an economic empire?" "Compare the way Athens chose its leaders with the way we choose ours." Occasionally the children are asked to make up sample questions for their social studies tests. On an occasion when the investigator was present the social studies teacher rejected a child's question by saying, "That's just fact. If I asked you that question on a test, you'd complain it was just memory! Good questions ask for concepts."

In social studies—but also in reading, science, and health—the teachers initiate classroom discussions of current social issues and problems. These discussions occurred on every one of the investigator's visits, and a teacher told me, "These children's opinions are important—it's important that they learn to reason things through." The classroom discussions always struck the observer as quite realistic and analytical, dealing with concrete social issues like the following: "Why do workers strike?" "Is that right or wrong?" "Why do we have inflation, and what can be done to stop it?" "Why do companies put chemicals in food when the natural ingredients are available?" and so on. Usually the children did not have to be prodded to give their opinions. In fact, their statements and the interchanges between them struck the observer as quite sophisticated conceptually and verbally, and well-informed. Occasionally the teachers would prod with statements such as, "Even if you don't know [the answers], if you think logically about it, you can figure it out." And "I'm asking you [these] questions to help you think this through."

Language arts emphasizes language as a complex system, one that should be mastered. The children are asked to diagram sentences of complex grammatical construction, to memorize irregular verb conjugations (he lay, he has lain, and so on . . .), and to use the proper participles, conjunctions, and interjections in their speech. The teacher (the same one who teaches social studies) told them, "It is not enough to get these right on tests; you must use what you learn [in grammar classes] in your written and oral work. I will grade you on that."

Most writing assignments are either research reports and essays for social studies or experiment analyses and write-ups for science. There is only an occasional story or other "creative writing" assignment. On the occasion observed by the investigator (the writing of a Halloween story), the points the teacher stressed in preparing the children to write involved the structural aspects of a story rather than the expression of feelings or other ideas. The teacher showed them a filmstrip, "The Seven Parts of a Story," and lectured them on plot development, mood setting, character development, consistency, and the use of a logical or appropriate ending. The stories they subsequently wrote were, in fact, well-structured, but many were also personal and expressive. The teacher's evaluative comments, however, did not refer to the expressiveness or artistry but were all directed toward whether they had "developed" the story well.

Language arts work also involved a large amount of practice in presentation of the self and in managing situations where the child was expected to be in charge. For example, there was a series of assignments in which each child had to be a "student teacher." The child had to plan a lesson in grammar, outlining, punctuation, or other language arts topic and explain the concept to the class. Each child was to prepare a worksheet or game and a homework assignment as well. After each presentation, the teacher and other children gave a critical appraisal of the "student teacher's" performance. Their criteria were whether the student spoke clearly, whether the lesson was interesting, whether the student made any mistakes, and whether he or she kept control of the class. On an occasion when a child did not maintain control, the teacher said, "When you're up there, you have authority and you have to use it. I'll back you up." . . .

The executive elite school is the only school where bells do not demarcate the periods of time. The two fifth-grade teachers were very strict about changing classes on schedule, however, as specific plans for each session had been made. The teachers attempted to keep tight control over the children during lessons, and the children were sometimes flippant, boisterous, and occasionally rude. However, the children may be brought into line by reminding them that "It is up to you." "You must control yourself," "you are responsible for your work," you must "set your own priorities." One teacher told a child, "You are the only driver of your car—and only you can regulate your speed." A new teacher complained to the observer that she had thought "these children" would have more control.

While strict attention to the lesson at hand is required, the teachers make relatively little attempt to regulate the movement of the children at other times. For example, except for the kindergartners the children in this school do not have to wait for the bell to ring in the morning; they may go to their classroom when they arrive at school. Fifth graders often came early to read, to finish work, or to catch up. After the first two months of school, the fifth-grade teachers did not line the children up to change classes or to go to gym, and so on, but, when the children were ready and quiet, they were told they could go—sometimes without the teachers.

In the classroom, the children could get materials when they needed them and took what they needed from closets and from the teacher's desk. They were in charge of the office at lunchtime. During class they did not have to sign out or ask permission to leave the room; they just got up and left. Because of the pressure to get work done, however, they did not leave the room very often. The teachers were very polite to the children, and the investigator heard no sarcasm, no nasty remarks, and few direct orders. The teachers never called the children "honey" or "dear" but always called them by name. The teachers were expected to be available before school, after school, and for part of their lunchtime to provide extra help if needed. . . .

The foregoing analysis of differences in schoolwork in contrasting social class contexts suggests the following conclusion: the "hidden curriculum" of schoolwork is tacit preparation for relating to the process of production in a particular way. Differing curricular, pedagogical, and pupil evaluation practices emphasize different cognitive and behavioral skills in each social setting and thus contribute to the development in the children of certain potential relationships to physical and symbolic capital,[11] to authority, and to the process of work. School experience, in the sample of schools discussed here, differed qualitatively by social class. These differences may not only contribute to the development in the children in each social class of certain types of economically significant relationships and not others but would thereby help to *reproduce* this system of relations in society. In the contribution to the reproduction of unequal social relations lies a theoretical meaning and social consequence of classroom practice.

The identification of different emphases in classrooms in a sample of contrasting social class contexts implies that further research should be conducted in a large number of schools to investigate the types of work tasks and interactions in each to see if they differ in the ways discussed here and to see if similar potential relationships are uncovered. Such research could have as a product the further elucidation of complex but not readily apparent connections between everyday activity in schools and classrooms and the unequal structure of economic relationships in which we work and live.

---

11. *physical and symbolic capital*: Elsewhere Anyon defines *capital* as "property that is used to produce profit, interest. or rent"; she defines *symbolic capital* as the knowledge and skills that "may yield social and cultural power.